PUFFIN BOOKS
JAWAHARLAL NEHRU

Aditi De is a Bangalore-based author, dreamer, traveller, editor (though not necessarily in that order). She loves children and the world of the word. In 1989, she launched *Junior Quest*, the popular magazine from the Chandamama group, and later edited the *Open Sesame* children's supplement at the *Deccan Herald*. Her books include *A Twist in the Tale: More Indian Folktales* (Puffin India). She has written children's columns for *Chatterbox* magazine, *Deccan Chronicle* and *Young World*.

JAWAHARLAL
Nehru
THE JEWEL
OF INDIA

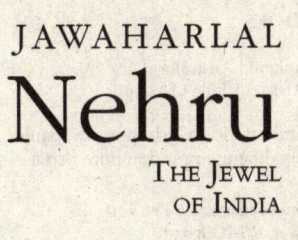

ADITI DE

PUFFIN BOOKS

An imprint of Penguin Random House

PUFFIN BOOKS

USA | Canada | UK | Ireland | Australia
New Zealand | India | South Africa | China | Singapore

Puffin Books is part of the Penguin Random House group of companies
whose addresses can be found at global.penguinrandomhouse.com

Published by Penguin Random House India Pvt. Ltd
4th Floor, Capital Tower 1, MG Road,
Gurugram 122 002, Haryana, India

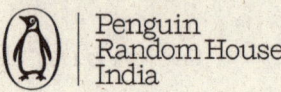

First published in Puff in by Penguin Books India 2009

10 9 8 7 6 5 4 3

ISBN 9780143330820

Typeset in Bembo by Eleven Arts, New Delhi

Printed at Repro India Limited

www.penguin.co.in

For Mehdi, Shruti, Tejas and Riyaz,
who light up my world with their lives!

Contents

1 ✍ Child's Play

This is the story of a man who marched alongside Mahatma Gandhi in the fight for Indian independence.

This is the journey of the first Prime Minister of independent India.

These are tales about a child born and brought up in Allahabad under the British Raj, who dreamt a big dream, for himself and for his country.

★ ★ ★

Jawaharlal entered his father Motilal Nehru's study quietly. He loved its warmth in the cold Allahabad winter, the whiff of leather-bound books on its shelves. He looked around, at the rich Kashmiri carpets on the floor, the vase of fresh flowers on a marble stand in a corner. Suddenly, a glittering object on the office desk caught his eye. Just about five or six years old then, Jawaharlal clambered on to Motilal's chair. He reached for the shiny, beautiful black fountain pen, trimmed with gold.

An only child, he was tired of playing on his own, bored with the toys his doting parents showered on him. He knew the pen had come from far, far away, across the seas. Maybe from England. In another corner of the desk, he spied another fountain pen. Why, Jawaharlal asked himself, would his father need two pens. So, without a second thought, he slipped the almost-hidden one into his pocket. For the next few hours, he did not write a word with it. He kept touching it, feeling its cool finish against his fingers. He had watched Motilal write long legal documents with his pen. One day, Jawaharlal dreamt of being just like his father, down to the big, booming laugh that resounded through the rambling house.

Quietly, the child played in a corner of the veranda. Suddenly, he heard a commotion from the study. The servants were summoned. He heard his father's voice raised in anger. He saw Munshi Mubarak Ali, the grey-bearded retainer with gentle eyes, talking firmly to all the staff.

As an adult, Jawaharlal remembers what happened later in his autobiography:

'I found a mighty search was being made for the lost pen and I grew frightened at what I had done, but I did not confess. The pen was discovered and my guilt proclaimed to the world. Father was very angry and gave me a tremendous thrashing. Almost blind with pain and mortification at my disgrace I rushed to Mother, and for several days various creams and ointments were applied to my aching and quivering little body.'

★ ★ ★

On another occasion, Motilal had invited some friends over, as he did quite often. They talked about the British, who ruled over India then. Of how these foreigners would insult local people. Of how, when an Englishman killed an Indian, a British jury would let him go scot-free. Of how some compartments in trains were reserved for the British: these were carriages that no Indian could board, no matter how crowded the rest of the train was! Of how benches and even chairs in public parks and other places were set apart, so that no Indian or even Eurasian could occupy one.

Jawaharlal often hid behind a curtain, trying to make sense of these adult conversations. Were the British all bad people? He knew that he admired his English governesses and Motilal's British friends. When caught in the act of eavesdropping, Motilal would drag the boy out and settle him on his knee. Jawaharlal could thus listen in more closely, which confused him even more. In company, Motilal often enjoyed a drink of whisky in the richly-furnished living room. Jawaharlal recognized the golden liquid in his father's whisky decanter quite easily. But one day, he found his father sipping a bright red liquid—probably claret—instead. Horrified, Jawaharlal rushed to his mother to report that his father was drinking blood!

★ ★ ★

As a boy of seven or eight, Jawaharlal would go for a ride on horseback. He was accompanied by a trained *sawar* or groom from the cavalry unit then based in Allahabad. He once slipped and fell off the pony. The horse, a pretty one of part-Arab stock, trotted back to the Nehru home at Anand Bhawan without its rider. Motilal and his wife were in shock. What had happened to the light of their lives? All the adults, led by Motilal, set out in search of Jawaharlal. Their odd procession was made up of vehicles of all sizes and shapes. En route, they found the boy limping back home.

His mother embraced him, his father patted his dishevelled head. For days afterwards, Jawaharlal was treated as a hero within the family!

★ ★ ★

On special days, Jawaharlal would accompany his mother and aunts to the holy Ganga for a dip. Allahabad (called Prayag in ancient times) was the location where the Ganga and the Yamuna met the mythical Saraswati river. He was aware that his was the city that hosted the Kumbh mela, a gathering of millions of pilgrims and holy men from around India, held once every twelve years.

But festivals, more than rituals, lingered in the child's mind. He loved the water-play and colours that added gaiety to Holi, the flickering earthen lamps that made Diwali so mystical, the songs of joy at the birth of Krishna at midnight on Janamashtami and the dramatic processions and plays that brought to life the story of Rama during Dussehra. He was a little puzzled, though, by the more tragic events commemorated during the Muharram processions that marked the story of Hasan and Husain in distant Arabia. As Kashmiris, the Nehru family also celebrated special days such as Naoroz, the new year's day, according to the Samvat calendar.

The one day that Jawaharlal looked forward to all year round was, of course, his own birthday. Early in the morning, he was placed in a huge weighing scale, while wheat and other foodstuff was weighed against him. All these bags full of food were distributed to those less well off than the Nehru family. Dressed in new clothes later in the day, he received presents from his parents and others at Anand Bhawan. By evening, it was time for a party.

'My chief grievance was that my birthday came so rarely,' he later wrote. 'Indeed, I tried to start an agitation for more frequent birthdays. I did not realize then that a time would come when birthdays would become unpleasant reminders of advancing age.'

★ ★ ★

What were Jawaharlal's growing years like?

Jawaharlal was an only child for the first eleven years. His sisters, known to us as Vijayalakshmi Pandit and Krishna Hutheesing, were far too young to play with him as equals. That made him a rather lonely dreamer. He lived in an era without the Internet, without the iPod, without video games, or—imagine this—even TV! Jawaharlal was taught by governesses and private tutors for sixteen years. He was sent neither to kindergarten nor to primary school. And so, he often played on his own because the cousins who shared his home within the large joint family in Allahabad were much older than him; they were already at high school or university.

Where did the Nehru family come from? Around 1716, an ancestor named Raj Kaul, an eminent Sanskrit and Persian scholar in Kashmir, attracted the attention of the Mughal emperor Farrukhshiar after the death of Aurangzeb. He was invited to migrate to the imperial court at Delhi. The Kauls' home in Kashmir was located on the banks of a canal, which is called *nahar* in Kashmiri. Gradually, the family name changed to Kaul-Nehru (or the Kauls who lived by the nahar), then to just Nehru!

Remember the great uprising of 1857, the one also called the First Indian War of Independence or the Sepoy Mutiny in your history books? Jawaharlal's grandfather, Ganga Dhar Nehru, was the *kotwal* or chief police officer of the Emperor of Delhi for some years before the revolt. He died in 1861. Most of the family's land documents were destroyed during the uprising, thus snapping their connection with the Delhi court. So, Jawaharlal's uncles wound their way to Agra. That's where his father, Motilal, was born in May 1861. Ganga Dhar had passed away three months earlier.

The teenaged Motilal admired his older brothers Bansi Dhar and Nandlal enormously. The former worked for the judicial department of the British government, so he was seldom with the rest of the family. Nandlal was, for a while, the prime minister or diwan of Khetri, a princely estate in Rajputana. Later, he earned his living as a lawyer in Agra. When the local high court moved to Allahabad in Uttar Pradesh, so did he. Allahabad then became the home of the Nehru family.

Motilal first studied mainly Persian and Arabic, learning English much later. While at Muir Central College at Allahabad, he sat for his first exam, but was not sure about whether he had done well. So he decided to skip the rest! Instead, he went away to look at the Taj Mahal—and so he never graduated. He was later told that he had scored very good marks in that first paper.

At Muir, Motilal admired his British professors. They, in turn, liked his independent spirit. Influenced by them, Motilal became very Western in his lifestyle, like many upper-class Indians in a country where the East India Company set up its first permanent factory in 1612, and the British Raj began in 1857. Motilal dressed in the English manner, often ate English-style meals, and enjoyed an evening of English conversation and claret with his friends.

After serving as an apprentice at the district court in Kanpur, Motilal moved to the Allahabad High Court. He enjoyed nothing so much as a good fight, especially one of words. His reputation grew from day to day at Allahabad. With it came money, fame and success.

But a huge blow came Motilal's way soon after he shifted to Allahabad. His brother Nandlal died suddenly. Almost overnight, Motilal became the head of the joint family that resided in a house in a congested Allahabad lane. Its entrance was said to be haunted! Nandlal's sons, cousins of the extended family, the children of his father's sisters, all lived together. The family was held together by Motilal's mother, Jeevarani, a woman known for her iron will. At twenty-two, Motilal married Swaruprani Thussu, a tiny woman with skin like porcelain, and delicate hands and feet. The family led a comfortable and luxurious life, lacking nothing in terms of fine food, imported clothing and toys.

It was in this house that Jawaharlal was born on 14 November 1889. He lived there for the first three years of his life. When he was ten, the family shifted to a big, new house, which Motilal named Anand Bhawan. Set amidst a sprawling garden with well-trimmed lawns, the rambling mansion had wide verandas all around it, with a central courtyard that opened into its bedrooms. Its grand columns, arches and terraces were set off by the cupola atop the building. It included the luxury of a swimming pool, which was rare in those years. So were the electric lights that set the mansion apart from most of the neighbouring houses in Allahabad.

During the hot Allahabad summers, a tiered fountain in the courtyard cooled the house. Whenever Motilal hosted an open-air party at Anand Bhawan, blocks of ice and flowers were set afloat in the fountain. The sweet scent of the blooms would waft into the bedrooms.

While the Western-style parties were held in the reception rooms to the front of Anand Bhawan, a traditional Indian lifestyle was followed in the rest of the house. Where Swaruprani reigned, the family and visitors sat on the floor, cushioned by big bolsters and cushions, low stools and divans.

While Motilal ate in the modern dining room at regular hours, the rest of the family were served lunch with hot *phulkas* in their living quarters by a retinue of servants. But he did insist that the family should try and eat dinner together.

Jawaharlal, who felt totally at home in the water, had a dip in the pool many times over, especially during the long, hot summer days. His father was not as much at ease, but could swim a length of the pool, though usually with clenched teeth and much physical effort.

The boy, watching his father's friends try out their usually meagre swimming skills, delighted in innocent pranks. For instance, he often saw Dr Tej Bahadur Sapru, who was still learning the ropes at the Allahabad court, sitting on the pool's first step, in about fifteen inches of water. Jawaharlal took much delight in pushing and pulling those who were as frightened as Sapru! His merriment was that of a child.

Neither Motilal nor Jawaharlal dreamt at that juncture that Anand Bhawan would one day become a part of Indian history in the making.

★ ★ ★

At this point, the Nehru family had little to do with Indian politics. What was the world around like then? Let's look at the year 1889, for instance. Mohandas Karamchand Gandhi, just twenty, was studying law in London. Gustave Eiffel had completed the grand tower named after him in Paris. Japan, ruled by a line of emperors, had been granted a constitution. The Indian National Congress, launched by a Scotsman named Alan

Octavian Hume in 1885, had turned four. Its fourth session in Bombay was presided over by an Englishman named Sir William Wedderburn.

The cobra at Anand Bhawan

For many years, a cobra lived in one of the outhouses to the rear of Anand Bhawan. It bothered no one, silently gliding into the garden, then back into the wood pile in the outhouse. It became a part of the daily life of the Nehru family and their household staff, who paid little attention to it.

One day, a new servant joined the staff. As he walked back to his room, he spotted the cobra. Horrified, he picked up a stout stick and killed it at once. He felt proud of himself, sure he had done the family a good turn.

As the movement for Indian independence grew, the Nehrus began to live more simply. Their horses were sold. Expensive furniture was auctioned. Many servants were asked to look for other jobs.

The servants were puzzled by this twist of fate. Then, one of the oldest among them remembered the cobra that once lived in their midst. He decided that the decline in the family fortune was the price the Nehrus had to pay for its untimely end!

2 🪶 No School till Sixteen!

In the early photographs of Jawaharlal as a large-eyed boy, he doesn't seem mischievous or capricious. He is clad in strange outfits, to our eyes. In one, he wears embroidered pantaloons and a coat, bejewelled slippers on his feet, in another he dons a sailor's outfit, while in a third he's in a kilt, the skirt-like Scottish man's costume. We can only guess that Motilal thought these were proper outfits for a child brought up in the Western manner.

Believe it or not, Jawaharlal did not go to school till he was sixteen, when he was sent to the English public school of Harrow in Middlesex. Until then, Jawaharlal was taught at home by a series of English governesses or private tutors. Maybe Motilal felt that the local schools were not good enough for his only son. He was determined to provide Jawaharlal with the best education possible.

Only one of the tutors, a shy man of twenty-six named Ferdinand T. Brooks, made a lasting impression on the boy, then eleven. Brooks' mother was Belgian, his father Irish. Dr Annie Besant, a founder of the Theosophical movement and a champion of Indian self-rule, recommended Brooks to Motilal. Why? Because, as a young man, Brooks came to admire Indian philosophy. He even learnt enough Sanskrit to translate the Bhagavad Gita.

Brooks and Jawaharlal spent hours rigging up a laboratory in which they tried scientific experiments. Isn't it easier to remember what you've seen before your own eyes or tried on your own, than what you've merely read on a printed page? No wonder, as Prime Minister, Jawaharlal wanted India to make great progress in scientific research and be equal to the rest of the world of science.

Through Brooks, Jawaharlal came to be fascinated by the ideas behind theosophy. In his tutor's room, amidst a gathering of adults, the boy would listen to new ideas. These would be about reincarnation or being born as another being as a result of our karma or actions in the present life. They talked about supernatural bodies and invisible *chakras* or auras, about thinkers as celebrated as the Buddha or Pythagoras (remember his theorem about the right-angled triangle?). The theosophists loved to talk about the nature of the soul and God. To the teenager, it sounded as if all the mysterious and fascinating secrets of the universe were being revealed to him.

At night, Jawaharlal dreamt of flying vast distances through the sky. As he flew, the countryside beneath revealed itself as a painted canvas. He imagined the mysterious life of an astral body. Did he think of himself as a meteor or a shooting star?

When Annie Besant addressed an audience in Allahabad, Jawaharlal was enchanted by her oratory, her magical way of making real a philosophy that was hard to pin down. Though just thirteen, he went to Motilal and asked if he could sign up for the Theosophical Society. He did not know then that his father was once a member, too, years ago when Madame Blavatsky first set up the society. Once a member, Jawaharlal even attended the theosophical convention in Varanasi.

Did Jawaharlal learn only of the West and its ways? Not quite. An elderly pundit was called on to teach him Sanskrit and Hindi. A friend of the Nehru family recalls that, among the boy's Sanskrit texts, he spied a beautifully printed edition of the *Samaveda*!

Yet English ways and the English tongue were primary to Jawaharlal's life. He once noted that he knew as little Sanskrit as he did Latin, the classical language he was to learn at his first school in England, Harrow.

How closely did Motilal bond with his son? Since the father led an incredibly busy life as a lawyer, he rarely spent real time with Jawaharlal. But on occasions when he could get away, he would teach him the finer points of tennis or cricket—perhaps the right way to hit a backhand cross-court, or how to bowl a googly or glance a shot past the first slip! On a windy day in Allahabad, the duo would fly a kite together, tugging at its string as it tossed, whirled and danced in the sky above.

It was to his mother, Swaruprani, that Jawaharlal turned more often. She would never scold the boy. His sister, Sarup, was born when he was eleven (after marriage, Sarup was renamed Vijayalakshmi Pandit). He told his mother of his dreams of inter-stellar flight, though possibly a far cry from *Star Wars*. He shared with her his longing for a sibling, as his cousins at home were far older than Jawaharlal, and busy with their education, jobs and families.

Swaruprani recounted to her young son tales of wily jackals and adventures on the banks of the Dal Lake, besides stories from Indian mythology. When he was just three, she taught him to be proud of who he was in these words, 'Kashmir is the marvellous mountain region in the north of India. The mountaintops there are covered in white snow, and down below are beautiful fields of tulips and other flowers, but most of all tulips. We Kashmiris are a proud and ancient people.'

Jawaharlal's aunt, the widow of Nandlal, told him stories from the Ramayana, of Lav and Kush, Rama and Lakshman. On other days, his eyes lit up as he listened to tales from the Mahabharata, fascinated especially by the war between the Pandavas and the Kauravas at Kurukshetra. He imagined the city they fought over, probably on the old bed of the Ganga, north-east of Delhi.

Did this make Jawaharlal lonely as a child? Perhaps. But his world gained comfort from the presence of Munshi Mubarak Ali, who looked after the daily running of the Nehru household. Whenever the old family retainer, with his lined face, white locks and silvery beard was free, the boy would snuggle up and ask him a million questions. Maybe they discussed what birds said to each other as they chirruped and sang. Or how the stars came to be. Or tales of ancient families, or of a time when Mubarak Ali was a boy.

Mubarak Ali must have gained much from the child's warmth, too. His family had lost all during the 1857 mutiny, when British soldiers hanged his father before his mother's eyes. Gentle and understanding, the old man would often cuddle the child as he told him stories from the Arabian Nights or unfolded some less gory scenes from the mutiny. He was, without doubt, Jawaharlal's best friend during his growing years. As an adult, Jawaharlal recalls, 'The memory of him remains with me as a dear and precious possession.'

The Russo-Japanese war of 1904–05 shattered Jawaharlal's peaceful world when he was just fifteen. Looking back at it as an adult in 1932, he recalls in a letter:

> *Early in the twentieth century an event occurred which had a great effect on the mind of Asia. This was the defeat of Tsarist Russia by Japan . . . I remember well how excited I used to get when news came of the Japanese victories . . . (It was) a great pick-me-up for Asia.*

To Jawaharlal, the conflict was exciting because it was about an Asian country battling the might of a European power. He read all he could about Japan, devouring newspapers, magazines and books. He was especially thrilled by the Japanese legends and ghost stories of Patrick Lafcadio Hearn, the son of an Irish father and Greek mother, who became a Japanese citizen.

He was known as Kaozumi Yakumo in Japan. Delighted by Hearn's stories, Jawaharlal imagined himself fighting for a free India, probably with a sword in hand, just like the knights in the Japanese tales.

In 1905, World War I was still nine years away. Germany was already gearing up for an arms race with Britain. The British were led by the Liberal Party, with Sir Henry Campbell-Bannerman as their Prime Minister. King Edward VII was on the English throne. Women in the West were beginning to fight for their right to vote. On the roads of London, steam buses ran alongside hansoms and four-wheel cabs and one-horse broughams. In the thick of all this came a vehicle that travelled at an amazing speed—20 miles an hour. It was the motor car!

A good read!

As a boy, Jawaharlal's favourite authors were Sir Walter Scott, Charles Dickens, William Makepeace Thackeray and H.G. Wells.

The books he liked best included Sir Arthur Conan Doyle's Sherlock Holmes series, Lewis Carroll's *Alice in Wonderland*, Rudyard Kipling's *Jungle Books* and *Kim*, Anthony Hope's *The Prisoner of Zenda*, and George du Maurier's *Peter Ibbetson* and *Trilby*.

Which book made him laugh the loudest? Jerome K. Jerome's *Three Men in a Boat*.

3 ✍ Off to Harrow and Cambridge

It was in May 1905 that Jawaharlal left India for the first time. Along with his mother, his father and four-year-old sister Sarup, he set sail for England, for there were no airplanes at that time. The journey took weeks.

Once in England, Jawaharlal opened a newspaper on a train that connected Dover with London. It headlined the victory of Admiral Togo of Japan over the Russian fleet at Tsushima. That made the teenager very happy.

It was the best mood in which to step into a new life at the all boys' public school of Harrow in the Christmas term. Harrow, about 16 km from London, was founded in 1572 during the reign of Queen Elizabeth I. It originally took in only local boys from the neighbourhood, but later opened its doors to outsiders who could pay for their tuition.

The sixteen-year-old Jawaharlal found that he was one of four or five Indian students at Harrow. The others included Indian royalty, such as the sons of the Gaekwad of Baroda in Gujarat and the Maharaja of Kapurthala. The latter was often teased by the other students. He promised to have his revenge if they ever visited him in Kapurthala in Punjab. Of course, that was years before royalty and titles were abolished by Indian law in 1971.

Like other boys' schools in India, Harrow encouraged students who were good at cricket or football. Jawaharlal was 'never an exact fit,' as he admitted later. But he did sign up for the Harrow School Corps, a little like the National Cadet Corps or NCC in India. In one black-and-white photograph taken at that time, Jawaharlal stands slim and erect in his corps uniform, though his face looks tense under the shako cap, which was tall, peaked and cylindrical.

He was placed in the Headmaster's house, the largest of Harrow's residential 'houses'. His housemaster, the genial and kindly Reverend Edgar Stogdon, was popular with his wards.

About thirty-five years after Jawaharlal left Harrow, Stogdon wrote: 'Nehru was in the house—a very nice boy, quiet and very refined. He was not demonstrative but one felt there was great strength of character. I should doubt if he told many boys what his opinions were, or the masters with whom he had a good name, as he worked well and seldom (almost never) gave trouble.'

Unlike other schoolboys, Jawaharlal read newspapers every day. He wanted to know what was happening in the world, especially in the India he had left behind. So, his general knowledge was way ahead of the others. In class, when asked about the Liberal government in Britain, the Indian boy was the only one who could name the entire Campbell-Bannermann cabinet!

Remember Jawaharlal's scientific experiments with Brooks as his tutor? His fantasies of flight soared as Wilbur and Orville Wright made forty-five flights in 1905.

During the longest one, they travelled 39 km in half an hour! A year later, Alberto Santos-Dumont flew 228.5 metres in twenty-one seconds!

Enthralled by these exploits, Jawaharlal wrote to his father, promising to soon pay the family a weekend visit by air. But the age of super-aviation, the Concorde and sleeper-beds, was still a speck in the sky.

In an unusual letter to his son at Harrow, Motilal wrote from Paris: *In you we are leaving the dearest treasure we have in this world and perhaps in other worlds to come . . . It is not a question of providing for you, as I can do that, perhaps from a single year's income. It is a question of making a real man of you, which you are bound to be. It would be extremely selfish, I should say sinful, to keep you with us and leave you a fortune in gold with little or no education . . . I never thought I loved you as much as when I had to part from you . . .*

Responding, Jawaharlal wrote to Motilal: *My dear Father, how I wish to be near you again. I wish the days would pass quicker and bring the happy day when I shall see you again . . .*

While at Harrow, Jawaharlal won a prize. It was one of G.M. Trevelyan's three volumes about Garibaldi, who led the struggle for Italian freedom. Enthralled, the boy got himself copies of the next two volumes. He saw how Indian culture had an impact throughout Asia, just as the Italian influence spread through Europe. He saw Rome and Varanasi as cities alike, central to the larger world around. If Italy could wage a battle that it won, could India do the same, he wondered.

The British dailies told the teenager little about the ferment in India. But he learnt of the boycott of British goods, of the move to support homemade or swadeshi products. Jawaharlal knew that Bal Gangadhar Tilak, who declared 'Swaraj is my birthright and I will have it,' was on the warpath against the more peaceful plans of the Indian National Congress. In Maharashtra, Tilak revived the Ganesha festival in a big way, uniting Indians through an icon they believed in. To the east, in Bengal, the cult of Kali was revived as leaders opposed the first partition of the state in 1905 (which was reversed in 1911), led by Bepin Chandra Pal and Cambridge-educated Aurobindo Ghosh (who later set up the famous ashram at Pondicherry). To the north, there were riots and protests in Punjab, led by Lala Lajpat Rai, known as 'the lion of Punjab.'

During holidays, Jawaharlal would meet other Indian students. They exchanged notes on their faraway homeland with deep emotion. 'All this stirred me tremendously but there was not a soul in Harrow to whom I could talk about it,' he wrote as an adult, looking back.

Jawaharlal loved the songs he learnt at Harrow. Later, at Anand Bhawan, he kept a book full of his scribbles of the words, and sang them aloud to nieces, nephews and grandchildren. His favourites included 'Jerry, You Duffer and Dunce' and 'When Grandpapa's Grandpapa was in the Lower Lower First'!

Five years after India gained independence, Jawaharlal was in London to attend the Commonwealth Conference in 1952. He took some time out to attend a dinner for old students of Harrow or Harrovians. Among them was Sir Winston Churchill, whose British government had—ten years before—sent the young Indian freedom fighter to jail for his last, yet longest, term.

What thoughts jostled through their minds as, over dinner, their voices sang these words of the old Harrow song together?

Forty years on, growing older and older,
Shorter in wind as in memory long,
Feeble of foot and rheumatic of shoulder,
What will it help us that once we were strong?

Once he was through with Harrow, eighteen-year-old Jawaharlal went to Trinity College at Cambridge University to study the Natural Science Tripos of chemistry, geology and botany. The university was then known for natural science, economics and philosophy. At the university's Cavendish laboratory, Sir J.J. Thomson was researching how electricity is conducted through gases, the charge and mass of the electron, and the analysis of positive rays. Jawaharlal was still as interested in science as he was when conducting those early scientific experiments in Allahabad with Brooks.

Always a reader, Jawaharlal was fascinated by Meredith Townsend's *Asia and Europe*, connecting him to his Indian identity via Asia. He also immersed himself in reading poetry by W.H. Auden, John Masefield, Walter de la Mare, Stephen Spender, T.S. Eliot and W. B. Yeats.

Harrow tidbits

Harrow was to gain fame as the school that gave Britain seven Prime Ministers, including Robert Peel (1834–46), Henry John Temple Palmerston (1855–65) and Winston Churchill (1951–1955). The poet Lord Byron and the playwright Terrence Rattigan also studied there.

Today, the original school is spread over 400 acres, including cricket fields and tennis courts, a golf course, woodlands and gardens. Its official colours are blue and white. The school has eleven 'houses' for its boarders.

In Harrow slang, a bath or shower is known as a 'tosh', while a teacher is sometimes referred to as a 'beak'!

In 1998, Harrow set up a school in Bangkok (Thailand), followed by another at Beijing (China) in 2005.

4 ✒ First Steps in Politics

On his return to India at the age of twenty-three, Jawaharlal found that the mood on its streets had changed dramatically. Like his father Motilal, he first came to admire Gandhi for a simple reason. The Mahatma was a man of action. They had been part of the Indian National Congress for years. But the party seemed to do little, apart from listening to long speeches from its leaders and passing resolutions. Could that possibly throw off the British yoke?

Motilal, as a lawyer, had always believed that rules in law books were above dispute. It disturbed him when his son fell under the spell of the Mahatma, who asked his followers to break 'unjust laws', even if that meant a spell in jail. He felt sick at heart that his son, from a proud aristocratic family, should even consider the idea.

One day, as the family waited for dinner, Jawaharlal walked into the Anand Bhawan drawing room holding a thick piece of twine. He twisted it this way and that, then created a loop that he put around his neck. Eyes twinkling, he said, 'I wonder what it feels like to have a noose around one's neck?'

Swaruprani nearly fainted. An angry Motilal stormed out of the room, slamming the door behind him. Others watched Jawaharlal in stunned silence. When dinner was announced, he quipped, 'Has this family no sense of humour left? Let's go and eat!'

Worried in ways he could not express, Motilal secretly tried sleeping on the floor of his own bedroom that night, to experience what his son might have to go through.

All around them, history was moving at a quick pace. In June 1917, the British detained Dr Annie Besant. She was a British theosophist who had set up the Home Rule League nine months before this. She supported an India for Indians. Motilal joined her group.

Meanwhile, World War I raged in Europe from 28 June 1914, when Austrian Archduke Franz Ferdinand was assassinated by a Bosnian Serb nationalist Gavrillo Princip. Within weeks, most European countries were at war through a series of alliances. When a peace treaty was finally signed on 28 June 1919, after an Allied victory, the battlegrounds extended to Africa, the Middle East, the Pacific islands and briefly China. Germany, Russia, Austria–Hungary and the Ottoman empire no longer existed. The Soviet Union came to be from the debris of the Russian empire. Over 22 million people lost their lives.

How did the Congress come into the lives of the Nehrus? It all began when the British came up with the Rowlatt Act in March 1919, which allowed them to arrest, try and imprison Indians without going by the law. Riots broke out to protest against this. Shortly afterwards, British General Reginald Dyer led his troops to fire 1,605 rounds of ammunition on a crowd of unarmed Indians at the Jallianwalla Bagh in Punjab, killing 379 people, wounding at least 1,200.

The British government got even tougher after that. They insisted that all Indians should crawl on their bellies through an Amritsar street where an English woman had been attacked by a mob. That hurt both Motilal and his son deeply. But the father still held back from joining Gandhi because that would mean giving up their luxurious lifestyle. Yet every day he saw his son drawn deeper into the Gandhian way.

While the family ate their elaborate Kashmiri meal in silver *thalis* and *katoris*, and drank from European crystal glasses, Jawaharlal began to reduce his personal needs. He asked to be served merely bread and milk at night. He ate this from a steel bowl, in preparation for jail in the future!

What drew Jawaharlal to the Mahatma, whom he differed from on the subject of the haves and the have-nots, political ways, and even economics? It was his courage. He watched with admiration as Gandhi preached that those oppressed could throw off the yoke of their masters once they had wiped out fear. He taught the masses to walk with their heads held high. He seemed able to read the hearts and minds of the common Indian.

Jawaharlal, who often used his head rather than his heart, was drawn to these qualities in the Mahatma. It was in 1916 that the two men met at the annual session of the Indian National Congress at Lucknow.

Nehru was then twenty-seven, while Gandhi was twenty years older. Jawaharlal had been back home from England for four years now.

Jawaharlal wore European clothes, as he had at Harrow and Cambridge, while Gandhi was clad in his coarse cotton dhoti, topped with a long coat and traditional Kathiawadi turban on his head. Jawaharlal seemed shy. He spoke with a clipped English accent. Much of what Gandhi preached seemed outdated to the younger man.

Did Gandhi take to Jawaharlal at once? Perhaps not, for his autobiography—*The Story of My Experiments with Truth*—which was written between 1922 and 1924, does not refer to the younger man even once.

This is what Jawaharlal wrote of that first meeting with Gandhi, 'All of us admired him for his heroic fight in South Africa, but he seemed very distant and different and unpolitical to many of us young men.'

It was the Rowlatt Act in 1919 that made the two Nehru men think alike. Before launching a non-violent satyagraha against it, Gandhi asked the Viceroy, Lord Chelmsford, to withdraw the unfair laws. But the British rulers paid no attention. What can we do about this, Congress leaders, including Motilal, asked Gandhi, when the Rowlatt Bills were being discussed. The Mahatma replied: We can offer satyagraha in protest.

To Jawaharlal, this seemed like the perfect answer: 'At last (there) was a way out of the tangle, a method of action which was straight and open and possibly effective.'

When the Viceroy refused to change his mind about the Rowlatt Act, Gandhi called on the country to mourn for a day through a *hartal*, when all business would come to halt. 30 March was the day chosen originally, but this was later postponed to 6 April.

Somehow, the news of the later date did not reach the organizers of Satyagraha Day in Delhi on time. And so, at Chandni Chowk in the old city, Hindus and Muslims came together to protest against these high-handed measures. At the Jumma Masjid, where the Emperor Aurangazeb had once prayed, Swami Shraddhananda addressed thousands of Muslims. The British were scared by such a show of unity in the capital. The army and police fired on some crowds.

Again, on 6 April, unarmed crowds in Amritsar, Lahore and Bombay were fired on. Angered, dozens of people attacked Europeans. There were blazes in public places, and riots broke out.

Gandhi was arrested as he travelled from Bombay to Delhi two days later, but was released on 10 April. But news of curbs on the Mahatma made the crowds in Bombay and Ahmedabad angry. They stoned vehicles and set some buildings on fire.

The Indian people had never before been called on to stage a protest across the country. Gandhi had his finger on their pulse just right.

By 15 April, martial law or the rule of the army took force in Punjab. The people there had a very tough time till it was lifted on 9 June. Anger swept through India in waves, more strongly then ever before since the 1857 rebellion in Lucknow (known as both the First Indian War of Independence and the Sepoy Mutiny).

Four Britishers and four Indians, headed by Lord Hunter, formed a committee set up by the rulers to look into what went wrong, especially after Jallianwalla Bagh. The Britons and the Indians could not agree about the causes, but all of them agreed that General Dyer was wrong. Later, he got an early retirement from the army. Oddly enough, the 'ladies of England' decided to present him with a golden sword, which only fanned the resentment in India even higher.

The happenings in Punjab brought Jawaharlal into the inner circle around Gandhi for the first time. The Congress Party, led by Swami Shraddhananda and Pandit Madan Mohan Malaviya, a key figure behind the Benaras Hindu University, set out to help those in distress in Punjab. As the party explored what really occurred there, Jawaharlal often visited Jallianwala Bagh with a leader from Bengal, 'Deshbandhu' Chittaranjan Das (the title means 'a friend of the country').

In late 1919, Jawaharlal records a train journey by night from Amritsar to Delhi. He found it impossible to sleep all night because a red-faced English general kept boasting about how he dealt with a crowd at Amritsar. At Delhi station, this person got off the train in what Jawaharlal recalls as bright pink striped pyjamas and a dressing gown. It was General Dyer!

Satyagraha

'Satyagraha' means holding firmly on to the truth. The word was first coined by Maganlal Gandhi in response to a contest in the South African journal *Indian Opinion* in 1906, when the Mahatma first began his non-violent protests there. It is based on two Sanskrit words, *satyam* (truth) and *agraha* (determination or insistence on).

Led by Gandhi, one of the first successful satyagrahas was carried out by people of Indian origin in South Africa in 1908. They were protesting against a law that required them to carry registration certificates at all times.

This method of fighting for rights was later used in movements around the world. Such struggles included the American civil rights movement in the 1960s led by Martin Luther King, the battle to free South Africa of apartheid, spearheaded by Nelson Mandela, and the Polish Solidarity struggle headed by Lech Walesa in the 1980s.

5 🪶 Marriage with Kamala

Three years before the events in Punjab, Jawaharlal married Kamala Kaul on Vasant Panchami in March 1916. It was the day when Saraswati, the goddess of learning, is worshipped with the coming of spring.

Kamala was about seventeen then, while he was twenty-six. A Kashmiri like him, she was tall, slim and pretty, with large, sparkling eyes. Though she had not been schooled for long, she was intelligent and not afraid to express her opinion. Among friends and the family, she could be gay, loving and full of fun. At other times, she could be shy among strangers, and outsiders sometimes thought she was cold.

How did Jawaharlal meet Kamala? Swaruprani, his mother, first saw her at a party. She was so charmed by her youth and loveliness that she made up her mind in a few minutes that this would be the right partner for her son.

Motilal, who adored his son, decided that only the finest he could afford would do for Jawaharlal's bride. He personally chose the precious stones for her ornaments. A little goldsmith's corner was set up in Anand Bhawan, where the stones were set in gold, to patterns chosen by Motilal whenever he could spare time from the courts. The jewellers often came to Anand Bhawan from Delhi or Bombay.

Since ladies from reputed families seldom went to the shops in those days, the finest silk, organza and brocade saris were brought to their home from all around Allahabad. Swaruprani chose the best for Kamala from these. A special train carried the family and their guests from Allahabad to Delhi, where the wedding took place.

When Kamala came home to Anand Bhawan and its rather rich lifestyle, it seemed like a palace to her. Its drawing room had gorgeous carpets from Persia, silver ornaments, delicate china from Dresden in Germany and sparkling glass objects from the island of Murano off Venice. Dozens of servants in uniform took care of their expensive cars and carriages, so that every Nehru could travel in comfort. The family's pet dogs were rather pampered too. Wealth could not have bought any more comfort.

Once married, Kamala often found her husband caught up in political life. He took his home and all its comforts for granted. He just had to ask for delicious food or a drive to a distant place for his wish to be granted. Kamala and Jawaharlal discovered they were quite alike. Often, they quarreled over minor issues. At first, he may have found her too direct, not as well read as he was. She seemed almost too simple, compared to the sophisticated Nehrus with their Western ways. He often thought that she did not understand all that was happening in India beyond their own doorstep.

On 19 November 1917, they had their first child, Indira Priyadarshini, who went on to become the Prime Minister of India when she was forty-nine years old.

Kamala's health began to fail shortly after. She later lost two children, including a son who survived only two days. Jawaharlal's mother had been similarly ill since he was born. Tending to Swaruprani and Kamala with great tenderness, he realized the value of good health, and of having a keen mind in a healthy body. From then on, he practised yoga every day, even when he was the Prime Minister.

In May 1920, Jawaharlal decided that his wife and mother needed a holiday to recover their health. He chose Mussoorie, a hill station in the Himalayan foothills. Guess who was staying in the same hotel as the Nehrus? An Afghan delegation. They wanted to negotiate peace with the British after their king, Amanullah, had gone to war against them briefly in 1919.

The British asked Jawaharlal to leave Mussoorie. They feared that the Afghans would get in touch with him, complicating matters. They asked Jawaharlal to promise he would not deal with them. He refused. So they asked him to leave the district within twenty-four hours.

When Motilal got the order reversed about a fortnight later, he took Jawaharlal back to Mussoorie. What did Jawaharlal see as he entered the hotel? His baby daughter Indira being carried around by an Afghan from the delegation, as she gurgled with delight.

All around the Nehrus, life was moving at an unusual pace. When Jawaharlal chose the politics of Mahatma Gandhi, Motilal made a life-changing decision in late 1920. He gave up his own practice as a lawyer at the bar. Now there was less money for the family to spend. He sold his carriages, then the horses that went with them. He sent most of his servants away. Like Swaruprani, Kamala learnt to give up the luxury of wearing silk and satin. Instead, the women wore saris of khadi and other garments of coarse linen from then on.

It was not always easy for Kamala to be part of the Nehru family. She was brought up in less Western ways than theirs. It was difficult for her when Jawaharlal was arrested and jailed for over 350 days during the independence struggle. Though she battled tuberculosis and a fierce racking cough for years before she passed away in February 1936, Kamala, too, came under the Gandhi spell. While she led a protest outside an Allahabad government college in 1931, she suddenly felt her knees buckle under her and fainted from fatigue. Among the young protesters who rushed to help her was Feroze Gandhi. He was to later marry Indira Gandhi, then a student at Shantiniketan, the school set up by Rabindranath Tagore in Bengal.

After Kamala passed away, Jawaharlal frequently looked back at their early years. He realized that he had often forgotten to talk to her, to eat with her, to even ask if she had eaten, so busy was he with all that was happening in India. Feeling sad about that, he wrote: 'She gave me strength, but she must have suffered and felt a little neglected. An unkindness to her would almost have been better than this semi-forgetful casual attitude.'

The khadi wedding sari

When Indira Priyadarshini Nehru and Feroze Gandhi got married at Anand Bhawan on Vasant Panchami in 1941, she wore a very special sari. It was made of khadi, woven from yarn spun by Jawaharlal Nehru while he was in jail, and dyed in the traditional Kashmiri wedding colour of pink. Indira wore no jewellery, only flowers in her hair.

On 28 February 1968, Indira's older son Rajiv Gandhi married Sonia Maino in Delhi. It was Vasant Panchami again. The bride wore the same pink sari. When their daughter, Priyanka Gandhi, married Robert Vadra in Delhi on 18 February 1997, this sari, woven by her great-grandfather, was what the bride wore.

Many years before this, Swaruprani wanted her older daughter Sarup to be married in fine brocade. Motilal was not happy with this. One day, the bride-to-be received a parcel from the Mahatma, containing six yards of the finest khadi woven by his wife, Kasturba. Dyed in pink, the bride wore this unique sari with pride, while her jewellery was made of flowers!

The charkha, or the spinning wheel, and the khadi yarn that was produced from it, was a symbol of Indian pride since 1921. During the independence struggle, Mahatma Gandhi encouraged Indians to make bonfires of foreign fabric and clothes, and to wear their homespun khadi clothes as a sign that they would throw off the British yoke.

6 🪶 A Man of the Masses

Back in Allahabad from Mussoorie in May 1920, Jawaharlal discovered what he liked best of all in politics. 'I like to open my heart to the crowd,' he later wrote.

He decided to visit about 200 farmers on the banks of the Yamuna, who were led by Baba Ramchandra, the peasant leader from Avadh, now in Uttar Pradesh. They were planning a march on Allahabad because the landlords they worked under often cut their wages or bullied them. They begged Jawaharlal to visit their village, to check out the truth of their lives.

He took a few companions with him. They all stayed at a village for three days. That experience changed his life. For the first time, he saw villagers who had no clothes, except mere rags. They rarely ate two square meals a day. Often, their bones showed through their skinny frames. He was horrified when local moneylenders cheated the uneducated peasants over and over again. He watched as they were beaten for working too little after they had toiled the whole day. He was appalled when they were thrown out of their huts, even off their land, without any justice.

From that time onwards, Jawaharlal's vision of India changed. He no longer saw it as a sea of city-dwellers who lived comfortable lives. Instead, he constantly thought of these poor men and women, and their children—who seldom went to school, who had so little to eat and never enough clothes to wear, even in the coldest of winters.

As he listened to their troubles, he wondered how he could help. Tired of their tough lives, they seemed to believe that Jawaharlal could set their wrongs right. Could he persuade them not to take their battles to court, settling them in the local panchayat instead? Could he ward off the tyranny of the landowners?

Jawaharlal visited dozens of villagers. He discovered a forgotten India. He listened to the farmers, heard the cries of their starving wives and children. He tried to teach them simple ways to improve their own lives, without taking the law into their hands. He encouraged them to take on the landlords without fear.

Later, Jawaharlal wrote of these experiences:

Looking at them and their misery and overflowing gratitude, I was filled with shame and sorrow, shame at my own easy-going and comfortable life and our petty politics of the city which ignored this vast multitude of semi-naked sons and daughters of India. A new picture of India seemed to rise before me, naked, starving, crushed and utterly miserable. And their faith in us, casual visitors from the distant city, embarrassed me and filled me with a new responsibility that frightened me . . .

Jawaharlal also understood now, that most Indian villagers may not have been to school, but they were incredibly intelligent. Most of them could recite verses from the Ramayana that they had learnt from their parents or grandparents. As he travelled, he would hear cries of 'Sita-Ram,' and found that hundreds would gather in a village in response to this call.

In the villages, Jawaharlal found that the Mahatma's message of non-violence had reached the masses. How did they use it? Around September 1920, hundreds of peasants gathered around a district jail, where some of their leaders were being held for a petty reason. The authorities, quite unused to such a show of local power, released those arrested after a quick trial. Jawaharlal was in Calcutta when he heard about this.

Excited by their success, the farmers decided to try the same tactic again after some time. But the British authorities were angry this time. The police fired on the crowd, killing a few. Jawaharlal tried to rush to the riverbank where he could hear shots, but he was stopped near a bridge by the police.

Soon, over 2,000 frightened villagers surrounded him. They were puzzled about why the Mahatma's methods had failed them this time. Speaking gently, Jawaharlal calmed them and sent them on their way home.

At this time, he was constantly followed by policemen, in case he stirred up trouble. Once, the man deputed to keep tabs on him was a puny, delicate young man who wore shiny, fancy shoes. Irritated by such a lack of freedom, Jawaharlal took to walking at a brisk pace, leaving his escort panting way behind.

The villagers were intelligent but, lacking much education, they were often taken advantage of by wily people. For instance, in the late 1920s, the servants of a landlord were told that the Mahatma wanted them to steal from another landlord. Unthinking, they did so, raising slogans of *Mahatma Gandhi ki jai*. Angry when he heard about this, Jawaharlal called on over 6,000 villagers to listen to him. He pointed out how wrong they had been, and how the Mahatma would probably be ashamed of them. Without thinking, he asked the leaders of this plot to raise their hands. Over twenty hands went up. In minutes, the police had swooped down on these farmers. Soon, hundreds, then a thousand peasants, were sent to prison.

The peasant or kisan unrest in areas like Avadh forced the British into action. In law, the son of each farmer was supposed to become the landlord's tenant after his father. But this seldom happened, until the peasant rebellions. Then the authorities moved quickly to see some justice done.

Did Jawaharlal, then, love the poor? On more than one occasion, he said, 'I hate poverty.' Yet, more and more, he began to find his heart reaching out to the downtrodden.

In his own words, 'I am vain enough in many ways, but there could be no question of vanity with these crowds of simple folk. There was no posing about them, no vulgarity, as in the case of many of us, of the middle classes, who consider ourselves their betters. They were dull certainly, uninteresting individually, but in the mass they produced a feeling of overwhelming pity and a sense of ever-impending tragedy.'

Jawaharlal, of course, was just one of thousands of city people who went to the Indian villages because Gandhi had called on them to find out more about the real India. At that point, neither he nor the others realized that their journey would shake up the subcontinent and the British empire.

Around him, Jawaharlal saw other signs that change was coming into Indian life. Motilal presided over the Amritsar session of the Congress in 1919. At first, Jawaharlal tried to be cautious because he knew his father was scared that drastic action could result in a jail term. But after Jallianwalla Bagh, even Motilal realized that Indians could take no more of British oppression. He backed Gandhi's call for the Satyagraha Sabha.

One major reason why Motilal made this difficult decision was because he could see where Jawaharlal's heart lay. But this cost him a lot in personal choices. When he chose not to use the foreign luxury goods the Nehrus were used to, he also had to turn away from his many British friends. He even had to pull out Jawaharlal's youngest sister, Krishna, from her British school!

Were both father and son equally under the spell of Gandhi? Perhaps not. Jawaharlal wrote, 'I was bowled over by Gandhi straight away. But with Father, it was different. He could not leap as I did. The process was long-drawn, even painful. Father was not the man to bend his will to anyone else's. But once he was convinced and had made up his mind, he never changed.'

On 1 August 1920, Gandhi returned all his British medals and awards to the Viceroy, Lord Chelmsford. These included the Kaiser-i-Hind gold medal for his contribution to ambulance services in colonial South Africa, and the Zulu war medal granted in 1906 for serving as officer-in-charge of the Indian volunteer ambulance corps there.

Ten days later, Jawaharlal and other Indians read what Gandhi wrote in the magazine called *Young India*:

'I do believe that where there is only a choice between cowardice and violence I would advise violence ... I would rather have India resort to arms in order to defend her honour than that she should in a cowardly manner become or remain a helpless witness to her own dishonour. But I believe that non-violence is infinitely superior to violence ...'

In 1920, millions of Indians listened to Gandhi who was yet to become a global legend. Throughout that year, he travelled around India, often accompanied by the nationalist and Khilafat movement leader Mohammed Ali and his younger brother Shaukat Ali, a journalist. They had pledged to support him. This made watchers realize how similar people of all religions were. Born of this, a cry was often heard around India: *Hindu Mussalman ki jai.*

At the Calcutta session of the Congress in September 1920, and the next one at Nagpur in December, the mood was different. The party no longer saw only members educated in British schools, who spoke mainly in English. More and more people who wore khadi with pride, who spoke in Hindi or other Indian languages, joined their ranks.

At Nagpur, the party decided to go with the Gandhian non-cooperation movement against the British. Even the law courts were to be boycotted. A startling event took place between these two sessions. The British called for elections to their new legislature in November. Gandhi called for non-cooperation. He asked the masses to boycott the poll. A British journalist, Valentine Chirol, wrote in *The Times* that from 8 a.m. till past midnight, not a single voter came to the polling booths!

At thirty-one, Jawaharlal felt caught up in a cause he believed in. 'We lived in a kind of intoxication during the year 1921. We were full of excitement and optimism and buoyant enthusiasm. We sensed the happiness of a person crusading for a cause.'

More and more, he found himself in the villages of the United Provinces (this covers Uttar Pradesh and beyond now). Jawaharlal surprised himself. He found it so easy to talk to the farmers, the weavers and the potters. Little by little, he tried to convince them that the Gandhian way could be the right path to swaraj or self-rule.

In July 1921, the Congress called on Indians to spin their own thread, weave their own cloth. It was a call to the charkha. They were asked to boycott the liquor shops, which made the government rich. On 31 July, there was a huge bonfire of foreign cloth in Bombay as Gandhi looked on. He thought that this move would get Congress leaders and workers back to the peasants, back to the true soul of India.

Many political messages of that time were spread by word of mouth. Rumours spread like wildfire, and often had to be squashed. When Jawaharlal's younger sister Sarup married a young lawyer named Ranjit Pandit on 10 May, people in the British areas whispered that the occasion was only a mask for political trouble. By coincidence, the day marked the anniversary of the Indian Mutiny of 1857!

As discontent rippled through the Indian subcontinent, the British made another move. They thought Indians would appreciate a royal visit, so they asked the Prince of Wales (later the Duke of Windsor) to make a state trip from 17 November 1921. The Congress, predictably, called on the country to boycott him.

The prince landed in Bombay to be greeted by riots that did not stop for three days, while buildings and vehicles were set on fire. The police fired on the teeming crowd. Over fifty people were killed, and more than 400 injured. Aghast, Gandhi went on a fast till peace was restored in Bombay. He broke it only on 22 December.

Wherever the prince travelled, he found that Indians did little to welcome or honour him. Schools were closed. Businesses shut their doors. Even the streets were deserted. Upset at this turn of events, the British decided to get tough in early December. They declared the Congress and its organizations illegal. They chose mass arrests, including that of the party's president-elect, Deshbandhu Chittaranjan Das. Even Indian government clerks, perhaps on their way home after work, found themselves in jail.

Did this break the spirit of those in search of swaraj? Not quite. Das left this message as he was led away: 'The whole of India is a vast prison. The work of the Congress must be carried on. What matters it if I am taken or left? What matters it if I am dead or alive?'

Like Mahatma Gandhi, Jawaharlal found himself on a road he had taken by accident, but one he began to love as he journeyed on. This was a path that led to his discovery of India.

Non-cooperation movement

This movement, launched by the Mahatma in September 1920, was aimed at bringing the British government to its knees. The Congress decided to support him at its Nagpur session that December. The movement lasted till February 1922.

The movement was in protest against the Rowlatt Act and the British move to send Indian soldiers into World War I without consulting the Indian people.

Indians were called on to stay away from British Raj-sponsored schools and colleges, to quit the military, police and civil services. Lawyers stayed away from British courts. Later, bonfires of foreign goods, including cloth, spread through the streets, as pride in khadi grew. British liquor shops were boycotted, as were stores that sold imported goods.

7 🕊 Jail, Again and Again

On 6 December 1921, Jawaharlal returned home to Anand Bhawan in Allahabad to find unusual activity. There were policemen all over the sprawling mansion. They had in hand two arrest warrants. One was for Motilal, for being part of the Congress volunteers, which the government had declared illegal. The other was for Jawaharlal, because he had passed around pamphlets calling for a hartal, a protest that closed down all offices and businesses, schools and colleges.

Did the Nehrus get a fair trial? Not exactly. Motilal's case rested on his membership of the Congress. An illiterate witness was brought in to swear that it was Motilal's signature on the membership form! As Motilal sat in the dock, Indira—who was then just four—sat on her grandfather's lap right through, wrapped in his arms.

Back home, Indira lined up her dolls and made fiery speeches to them. She called on them to court arrest. Her father had shown her it was noble to go to jail for India.

Since the Congress had decided to boycott the courts, neither father nor son offered any defence, though they were both lawyers. Once convicted, Motilal sent a message to his Congress co-workers. It said:

'Having served you to the best of my ability while working among you, it is now my high privilege to serve the motherland by going to jail with my only son. I am fully confident that we shall meet again at no distant date as free men. I have only one parting word to say— continue non-violent non-cooperation without a break until swaraj is attained. Enlist as volunteers in your tens and hundreds and thousands. Let the march of pilgrimage to the only temple of liberty now existing in India—the jail—be kept in an uninterrupted stream, swelling in strength and volume as each day passes.'

Between December 1921 and January 1922, over 30,000 Indians went to jail for political reasons: reasons like being Indian and wanting their homeland back.

Both Motilal and Jawaharlal were sent to the district jail in Lucknow. In the centre stood an old shed, about twenty feet by sixteen feet, where weavers once plied the shuttle and the loom. Sixteen of the new prisoners were confined there. The two Nehrus were lodged in a smaller shed within this space, along with two of Jawaharlal's cousins. All around them were huge barracks, where most other prisoners were confined.

Jawaharlal sometimes tended to the plants around their shed, watering them with tenderness. At other times, he fried eggs for his companions or made them some tea. In those days, the jailers were unused to such large numbers of prisoners. The rules were quite relaxed. The Nehrus were allowed to read as many newspapers as they wanted to. They learnt that despite the fact that Das was behind bars, the Congress held its session at Ahmedabad in 1921. Gandhi, still free, wore his famous loincloth for the first time at Ahmedabad. He urged

Indians to work towards swaraj through non-cooperation and non-violence. Throughout India, millions responded to Gandhi.

How did Jawaharlal spend his time in prison? He would spin on a charkha for an hour or so. Then he would help his companions to sweep and swab their new home. He even washed his own clothes, besides those of his father. He insisted that their surroundings be kept as spotless as possible. In the first few weeks, he taught Hindi and Urdu to those who had studied less than him. But this was later banned by the prison staff, who feared that the prisoners might conspire to rebel or even escape.

It was at Lucknow jail that his friends saw another side to Jawaharlal. Whenever any of them fell ill, he took care of them all night, soothing their brow with cool hands, making sure that they had enough water to drink or had the right medicines whenever possible.

Muriel Lester, a friend who visited him in jail on a hot day, found hornets buzzing around his cell. She asked if they troubled him. Smiling, he replied, 'At first, they bothered me a great deal. The window seemed alive with them. I kept killing them, but always new ones flew in to take the place of the slaughtered. After days of this warfare, I decided to try non-violence.' He mentally asked them to keep to their window, while he had the right to the rest of his cell. He reported no trouble at all from that day on.

Outside Lucknow jail, there was trouble at Chauri Chaura, which was in the Gorakhpur district of the

United Provinces. It all began when the police fired on a village procession. In anger, the mob set fire to the local police station, burning to death the twenty-two cops who had taken shelter there.

Aghast at this turn of events, Gandhi asked the nation to call off its widespread civil disobedience movement. Leaders all around him protested, but he would not listen to them. He stood firm by his belief in non-violence, no matter what happened. Reluctantly, the Congress had to back the Mahatma on 24 February 1922, though Motilal wrote a letter from jail disagreeing as a matter of principle.

Within days, and much to his own surprise, Jawaharlal found himself a free man after three months. Kamala was delighted to have her husband back at Anand Bhawan. Swaruprani was happy that her only son was with her, though her husband was still at Lucknow. But Jawaharlal felt odd to be a free man while all his other companions were still behind bars. He decided to hurry to Gandhi's side at Ahmedabad. Just the night before his arrival, the Mahatma was arrested and lodged in Sabarmati jail.

As Jawaharlal looked on at the trial, he was deeply moved by what he saw and heard. Pleading guilty, before being sentenced to six years in jail, Gandhi said, 'I believe that I have rendered a service to India and England by showing in non-cooperation the way out of the unnatural state in which both are living. In my opinion non-cooperation with evil is as much a duty as non-cooperation with good.'

Jawaharlal could hardly believe his ears as he heard the British judge, Sir Robert Broomfield, say to Gandhi, 'It is impossible to ignore the fact that you are in a different category from any person I have ever tried or am likely to have to try. It would be impossible to ignore the fact that in the eyes of millions of your countrymen you are a great patriot and a great leader ... If the course of events in India should make it possible for the government to reduce the period and release you, no one will be better pleased than I.'

While a free man, Jawaharlal kept busy trying to promote khadi and the boycott of foreign cloth. He was angry when he found that some big shops still sold such cloth on the sly. He tried to talk them into changing their ways, but drew no results. So, he called on Congress volunteers to stand outside these shops in protest, to picket them. Within six weeks, Jawaharlal was sent back to jail for a year and nine months. He was to be imprisoned by the British Raj seven more times.

Though he did not protest against this sentence, he had a few words for other Indians. He said:

Affection and loyalty are of the heart. They cannot be purchased in the marketplace, much less can they be extorted at the point of the bayonet. We are fighting for the freedom of our country and faith. I shall go to jail again most willingly and joyfully. Jail has indeed become a heaven for us, a holy place of pilgrimage.

But this time, it was different at the Lucknow jail. Motital had been shifted to hilly Nainital, and the rules were much stricter. Jawaharlal was confined to a stone-walled grey barrack in which he was forced to huddle alongside fifty others.

He tired easily of small talk. Walking round and round the barrack for exercise gave him no joy. He watched the skies, the clouds, the lashing monsoon rains. His eyes dwelt on the colours of the sunset. He was unused to bathing and washing and changing in a public place. Cloud-gazing almost turned Jawaharlal into a poet. He wrote, 'Sometimes, the clouds would break, and one saw through an opening in them that wonderful monsoon phenomenon, a dark blue of an amazing depth, which seemed to be a portion of infinity.'

Perhaps for the first time, Jawaharlal missed his family intensely. He imagined his mother at her daily routine in Anand Bhawan. He thought of Kamala, and the little ways in which she made life easy for him. And he thought of his little Indira Priyadarshini, whose second name meant 'dear to the sight' in Hindi. Nine years later, when he was in prison again, he wrote to her: 'Priyadarshini—dear to the sight, but dearer still when sight is denied.'

The jail was packed with men. He longed for the sound of women's voices, the peals of children's laughter. He once observed that he had not even heard dogs barking for months on end. Jawaharlal read constantly, devouring a range of books he might not have had the time to look at otherwise. He was denied any newspapers, so that he lost track of political events beyond the barred windows. Puzzled by this man who was deep in books at all hours, the prison's British superintendent once said, 'Mr Nehru, I cannot understand your passion for reading. I finished all my reading at the age of twelve.'

Often, the jailers found themselves at loggerheads with some prisoners. Disturbed by arguments with some of them, they decided to additionally punish those they thought were causing the trouble. The seven people they sent to a faraway corner of the jail included Gandhi's youngest son Devdas, Gandhi's secretary Mahadev Desai, and Jawaharlal. At long last, Jawaharlal found he had a little more space to himself.

The seven spun cotton on charkhas for a while. Then, two by two, they drew water from a well with a leather bag, a task originally allotted to yoked bullocks. They even grew their own vegetables. They ran around their cramped space for exercise.

On 14 November 1922, Jawaharlal spent his thirty-first birthday in prison. It was the first time this had happened, but similar birthdays lay ahead of him. During his last stint in jail in 1942, Jawaharlal observed to the Socialist leader Acharya Narendra Deva, 'Prison has made a man of me.'

Nehrus in jail

Jawaharlal and his father were not the only Nehrus to go to jail during the struggle for a free India. His frail mother Swaruprani was arrested, then held in Asansol in March 1933, when the banned Congress decided to hold its annual session at Calcutta. Kamala found herself behind bars on 1 January 1931, during the no-tax agitation, when Jawaharlal went on a hunger strike in Naini prison.

During the civil disobedience movement of 1932, Vijayalakshmi Pandit joined the millions who took to the streets in protest against the Raj. She was arrested on 27 January 1932, and sent to Lucknow jail for a year, along with her sister Krishna Hutheesing. Vijayalakshmi's youngest child, Rita, was only two-and-a-half then. Her husband, Ranjit Pandit, was also put behind bars in 1930.

In August 1942, Vijayalakshmi—who was later elected the first woman president of the United Nations General Assembly—was arrested once more during the Quit India movement. This time, she was lodged in Naini jail for nine months.

8 🖊 Congress Tug of War

When he was set free from jail on 31 January 1923, Jawaharlal found all was not well in India or in the Congress. Since Gandhi's arrest, two groups seemed to be fighting for power within the party. One group, which wanted to stick to the old programme of non-cooperation, had Motilal and Deshbandhu Chittaranjan Das as its leaders. The other, led by Chakravarti Rajagopalachari, who later became the second governor-general of free India, wanted to take part in the elections to the legislatures in order to get a majority. Neither was willing to agree with the other.

Upset by these squabbles, Jawaharlal decided to spend his time making the Congress in the United Provinces more efficient. Since the party had decided not to contest the legislative polls, his other choice was to have the party gain power through the municipalities. In time, he was to lead that body in Allahabad. Das was already the mayor of Calcutta. In Ahmedabad, Vallabhbhai Patel held that post, while in Bombay his brother Viththalbhai Patel held a senior municipal post. All of them belonged to the Congress.

Jawaharlal took care of the Allahabad municipality, with attention to every detail, for two years. At some point, he also became secretary of the Congress committee. He worked long and hard each day, often more than fifteen hours. By night, he was too tired to even eat well or sleep.

He turned down an offer from the British Chief Justice of the Allahabad High Court, Sir Grinwood Mears, to become the education minister of the United Provinces. Jawaharlal quickly realized that the British were trying to win his favour by giving him some power.

Thinking of all that Gandhi had set out to do, Jawaharlal felt the first stirrings of doubt. It seemed unclear to him what swaraj stood for. Did it mean that Indians should be allowed to rule themselves? Or that Indians should fight for complete independence? In his confused state of mind, Jawaharlal found his family the greatest source of comfort. In prison, he realized that he had not been especially kind to his wife. Slowly, it struck him that she wanted to fight the political battle for a free India alongside him.

After her early death on 28 February 1936, Jawaharlal wrote of the fragile, strong-willed woman, 'She wanted to play her own part in the national struggle, and not be a mere hanger-on and a shadow of her husband. She wanted to justify herself to her own self as well as to the world. Nothing in the world could have pleased me more than this, but I was far too busy to see beneath the surface and I was blind to what she looked for . . .'

If the party was torn by the tug of war within it, the ordinary Indian still seemed confident enough to find means of protest. For instance, over 2,000 people marched through Nagpur in central India in a 1923 satyagraha procession, carrying the Indian flag. From then on, the government decided to allow such peaceful flag marches.

But Jawaharlal was soon to be back in jail a third time. It was at a time when the Sikhs in Punjab offered non-violent protests again and again against the corrupt guardians of their shrines, the gurudwaras. No matter how many times the police beat them back with batons, new waves of volunteers kept coming to the fore. Jawaharhal was impressed by how they made Gandhi's idea work.

In Nabha, Punjab, the British had taken over power from the local king. They had appointed one of their own men to rule the state. Protesters gathered at Jaito, close by, to stage non-violent protests against this in 1924. Jawaharlal was invited to watch one of these marches. He arrived near Jaito with two others, only to be served with an order to leave. When Jawaharlal explained that they would not take part, but merely watch, the local policemen did not believe them. He placed them in the local police station for the night.

The next day, handcuffed to one of his companions, Jawaharlal was marched through the streets of Jaito to the railway station. Chained, they travelled in a third-class railway compartment to Nabha. They spent three days in a dirty jail cell there, where rats scurried all over their faces as they slept on the floor. Once they were free, all of them went down with typhus. Jawaharlal had to stay in bed for nearly a month.

Meanwhile, Motilal and Das had formed the Swaraj Party, which stood for council elections. They won a majority in the Central Legislature in December 1923. The Congress, at its Kakinada session in Andhra that year, had to recognize this. Its president, Maulana Mohammed Ali, insisted that Jawaharlal should become its secretary once more.

In January 1924, after serving two years of his six-year sentence, Gandhi was rushed to hospital in Poona for emergency surgery on his appendix. The British decided not to enforce the rest of his term. While Gandhi was recovering in Bombay, Motilal and his family visited him. Motilal asked him to persuade Jawaharlal not to endure physical sacrifices, such as living on parched rice and roasted gram, or travelling by third class on trains, even during the hottest of summer days. Gandhi said he would try his best.

Meanwhile, other events overtook Jawaharlal in his personal life. In 1925, Kamala fell very ill with tuberculosis. Treatment at a Lucknow hospital did not seem to help her. In March 1926, Jawaharlal decided to take Kamala to Europe for treatment. He sailed for Venice from Bombay with her. Indira, who accompanied them, was just eight then. They were to spend the next year and nine months away from India.

A flag is born

The Indian national flag did not always look the way it does today. Sister Nivedita, a disciple of Swami Vivekananda, came up with a red flag with a yellow inset in 1904. It had *Vande Mataram* inscribed on it in Bengali, with a symbolic thunderbolt which had a white lotus within it.

On 7 August 1906, Schindra Prasad Bose unfurled a tricolour at a rally against the Partition of Bengal at Calcutta's Parsi Bagan Square. Its saffron band had eight stars across it, with *Vande Mataram* across its white band, while a moon to the right and a sun to the left decorated the green band. This was known as the 'Calcutta Flag'.

The patriot Madame Bhikaji Cama hoisted another tricolour on 22 August 1907, at Stuttgart, Germany. In green, saffron and red, its eight lotuses on the top band stood for the eight British Indian provinces. *Vande Mataram* in Devanagiri script appeared on the middle band, while a crescent moon and a sun adorned the red band. It was jointly designed by her, Veer Savarkar and Shyamji Krishna Verma. It was popular with Indian revolutionaries based abroad, mainly in Berlin.

During the fight for Home Rule led by Bal Gangadhar Tilak and Anne Besant, a red and green flag made its appearance in 1917, with a Union Jack in the top left corner, and the Great Bear constellation across its green and red stripes.

At the 1921 Bezwada session of the Congress, Mahatma Gandhi unveiled another tricolour with the

charkha across all its bands. This was informally used by the party for the next decade. The Congress working committee did not approve of a saffron flag with a charkha on it at the Karachi session in 1931.

The Bombay Congress meet in August 1931 approved of a tricolour with a blue charkha on its white band.

It was on 15 August 1947 that the Indian flag as we know it—with the Ashoka Chakra at its centre—was first unfurled. It was based on the Indian National Congress flag designed by Pingali Venkayya.

9   To Europe ... and Back

The Nehru family had originally planned to stay in Europe for about seven months. But before they knew it, twenty-one months flew by. Most of their time was spent at Geneva in Switzerland, and at a sanatorium in Montana for Kamala's treatment.

During that spell, Jawaharlal's sister Krishna Hutheesing came to Europe to visit them in mid-1926. Later, Motilal joined them.

When Jawaharlal left Europe for home after college, he was just twenty-three. Much had happened in India and the world since then. Looking back at himself as a young man, he saw 'a bit of a prig, a queer mixture of the East and West, out of place everywhere, at home nowhere'. By 1926, he had grown into a man who was back in touch with his Indian roots, one who had learnt to step out of the boundaries of Anand Bhawan in Allahabad and reach out to the farmers and labourers in the vast India beyond.

Abroad, he found that the countries he had travelled to earlier had changed. The Soviet Union, the world's first communist nation, came into being in 1922. It had a huge impact on world politics until it ceased to exist in 1991. In 1926, Germany joined the League of Nations set up in 1920, mainly to prevent another outbreak of war. In Britain, coal miners went on a major strike, which fascinated Jawaharlal because he had finally begun to understand the minds of those brought up with less than he had.

In Europe, Jawaharlal understood that India had to see itself as a nation that was part of humankind, not just one struggling to throw off the British yoke. Some of these beliefs came to him through meetings with leading intellectuals of the time. Among them was the French writer Romain Rolland, who had written a biography of Gandhi. It was through him that Europe first came to know the Mahatma. This is how Rolland saw him: 'I saw surging up on the plains of Indus the citadel of the spirit which had been raised by the frail and unbreakable Mahatma. And I set myself to rebuild it in Europe.' Nehru met Rolland at Villeneuve in France, armed with a letter from Gandhi.

Jawaharlal also attended the Congress of Oppressed Nationalities at Brussels in 1927. There he met others who were to lead Asia into another era, such as Madame Sun Yat-sen, the first non-royal woman to become head of state as co-chairman of the Chinese Republic from 1968–72, then its President in 1981.

He also met some fascinating Indians who lived abroad. Among them was Raja Mahendra Pratap, who had travelled through much of Asia, including Afghanistan, Tibet and China. He visited Jawaharlal in an unusual outfit, the pockets of his jacket and trousers packed with letters, postcards and documents. Watching Jawaharlal's puzzled expression he explained, 'Long ago,

I lost a valuable dispatch box in China. Since then I have preferred to carry all my papers on my person.'

In Paris, he visited Madame Bhikaji Cama. Despite British attempts to disillusion Madame Cama, she continued championing the cause of India's freedom. A Parsi, this fiery woman was rather haggard, even gaunt, when she met Nehru. But her eyes were full of fire. Jawaharlal recalls that she came close to him and peered into his face, then bombarded him with questions without waiting for his answers! He soon realized that she was a trifle hard of hearing.

Whenever Kamala's health allowed him to take a break, Jawaharlal took some time out to visit Europe's beautiful monuments and enjoy its lovely scenery. He also did some skiing. One expedition to the Swiss Col de Voza led to a close shave with death. A tobogganing companion happened to push him down a snowy slope before he was ready. He was lucky enough to swerve away from a precipice in time and land on a rocky bed with just a few scratches.

It reminded Jawaharlal of an occasion shortly after his marriage when he was in Kashmir near the Zoji-la pass. On his way to the icy cave of Amarnath with a local guide, they crossed several glaciers, then faced an ice-field. Fresh snow lay all over it. As he stepped over a path, he felt it give way. He fell deep into a crevasse or a fractured glacier, but was pulled out by the rope that attached him to the others.

In 1927, Jawaharlal, Motilal, Kamala and Krishna travelled across Poland from Berlin to Moscow by train, at the invitation of the Soviet government. He noticed that Moscow had within it the ways of both the East and the West. He wrote, 'Asia peeps out of every corner, not tropical Asia but the Asia of the wide steppes and the cold regions of the north and east and centre. It has heavy boots on and every variety of long coat and hat.'

Away from the India of the bullock cart, Jawaharlal was puzzled by the droshky, a sort of horse-drawn rickshaw. 'Why should anyone use this ancient mode of locomotion it was difficult to imagine,' he asked himself as the Nehrus visited the opera and the ballet over four days.

Besides such luxurious sites, Jawaharlal also visited a prison just outside Moscow. He was impressed to find that though it housed political prisoners, most of the jail guards were unarmed. Only the two guards at the entrance carried bayonets.

During his long break in Europe, Jawaharlal was never unaware of the pulse of India. He was aghast when a Muslim fanatic murdered Swami Shraddhanand in December 1926. Gandhi continued to travel across the length and breadth of the country, asking people to be kinder to the oppressed, such as those labelled the 'untouchables', and asking them to prefer khadi to other fabrics.

In Britain, Prime Minister Stanley Baldwin's government decided to take a major step. On 8 November 1927, it appointed a commission headed by Sir John Simon to see whether the Indian government could be run differently. It was a body made up of only Britons, excluding Indians. Both Congress and the Muslim League were angry about this. In the Indian streets, even the common man was ready to rise in protest against such an insult.

Jawaharlal learnt of the Simon Commission while reading a newspaper in Moscow. He felt India needed him to return. In early December, the Nehru family set sail for Colombo from the French port of Marseilles. He found an India full of fire and storm on his arrival. At the 1927 Congress session at Madras, he put forward a resolution before the party which defined complete national independence as its target. Though Gandhi seemed unhappy about this, most party members went along with Jawaharlal.

Did Gandhi fear that Jawaharlal was drifting away from him in his politics? Perhaps. In a letter dated 17 January 1928, he wrote to the younger leader:

> *The differences between you and me appear to be so vast and so radical that there seems to be no meeting ground between us. I cannot conceal from you my grief that I should lose a comrade so valiant, so faithful, so able and so honest, as you have always been; but in serving a cause, comradeships have got to be sacrificed. The cause must be held superior to all such considerations. But this dissolution of comradeship in no way affects our personal intimacy. We have long become members of the same family, and we remain such, in spite of grave political differences.*

Jawaharhal kept his mind focused on the mood of the Indian people throughout 1928, aware of the stirrings of discontent all around. He remembered that, before he left for Europe, he had felt most at home among the farmers and workers. He wondered how he could help them now. He found a clue from a peasant uprising at Bardoli in Gujarat, led by Sardar Vallabhbhai Patel. They were protesting against the Bombay government's decision to hike their land taxes by 22 per cent.

Patel got the peasant landlords to rise against this tax, which they could not afford to pay. He organized them into sixteen different groups. The British government, angry about this, arrested the 250 volunteers who dared to challenge its might. It took away their plots, and auctioned them at very low prices. As the peasants looked to him for a solution, Patel said, only half-joking, 'Don't worry. Let the government take your land to England, if they can ...' In time, the government was forced to order an inquiry. The result? The tax was reduced to 5.7 per cent.

Jawaharlal was impressed that the British government could be beaten by such a stubborn, yet non-violent form of protest. He realized once more that Gandhi was on the right track.

An angry India greeted the Simon Commission when it arrived in Bombay on 3 February 1928. Wherever they went, they were greeted with crowds waving black flags and shouts of 'Simon, go back!'

The police had to fire on crowds at Madras and Bombay. At Lahore, another leader, Lala Lajpat Rai, was felled by the baton of a British officer, who hit him hard on his chest and shoulders. He had been standing by the road when he felt the first blows. The protesters he led were non-violent. Nine days later, he was dead. India reeled from the shock of this loss.

Not long afterwards, Jawaharlal himself faced the brunt of British brutality for the first time. At Lucknow, he was trying to get the Congress volunteers to protest against Simon, who arrived by train. Processions had been banned. So, several thousand protesters decided to walk to the meeting place in smaller groups of just sixteen.

Leading one group, Jawaharlal heard the sound of hooves bearing down on them. Looking back, he found a formation of over thirty-six policemen gaining ground on them. The horses reared their legs in the faces of the Congress volunteers. Their hooves quivered just above the unprotected heads of the Indians.

Scattered by the horses, the men ran towards the sidewalks, where the police beat them harshly with lathis or batons. When they were done, the street was filled with figures on the ground. Some had head injuries, others had broken limbs.

Jawaharlal decided to show he was unafraid. He stood quite alone, right in the middle of the road. Before he knew what was happening, he received two knocks across his back from the baton of a mounted policeman.

How did he feel at this first encounter with violence? He wrote, 'The bodily pain I felt was quite forgotten in a feeling of exhilaration that I was physically strong enough to face and bear lathi blows. And a thing that surprised me was that right through the incident, even when I was being beaten, my mind was quite clear and I was consciously analysing my feelings.'

As blows rained on him, Jawaharlal noted a desire to fight back, but he quickly recalled Gandhi's advice. Thinking back to the hatred on the faces of the British officers then, he wrote, 'But long training and discipline held. I did not raise a hand, except to protect my face from a blow. Besides, I knew well enough that any aggression on our part would result in a ghastly tragedy, the firing and shooting down of large numbers of our men.'

Were the faces of the Congress workers just as flushed with anger and hatred at this injustice, he asked himself later.

Events began to move at a quicker pace. Deputy superintendent of police Saunders, who reportedly beat down Lala Lajpat Rai, was shot to death in Lahore. He was the wrong target, though. As Simon sat in a gallery, two crude bombs exploded in the Central Assembly in Delhi. Bhagat Singh from Punjab was later sentenced to death for the Saunders killing.

Motilal, back from Europe, chaired the Calcutta Congress session in 1928. Jawaharlal still stood by his call for complete Indian independence, which made his father quite cross. At Anand Bhawan, there were arguments about political issues every day. Motilal found that he could do little to change his son's mind. Kamala supported her husband in these disagreements.

This made Jawaharlal think back to 1917 when he wanted to follow Gandhi, much against Motilal's wishes.

Once, in anger, his father ordered him out of their home. About to step out, Jawaharlal felt his new bride's cool hand slip into his. Motilal, watching his son and his daughter-in-law united against his anger, quickly changed his mind.

Shaheed Bhagat Singh

Bhagat Singh was born to a Jat family at Khatkar Kalan village in Punjab in September 1907. Like his grandfather Arjun Singh, he was a keen follower of the Arya Samaj movement. Arjun Singh refused to allow the boy to attend the Khalsa High School in Lahore, because it taught loyalty to the Raj. So, Bhagat attended the Dayanand Anglo Vedic High School instead.

At thirteen, Bhagat Singh decided to follow the Mahatma's non-cooperation movement. He burnt his government school books and imported clothing. But he was upset when the movement was withdrawn after the Chauri Chaura incident in the United Provinces on 4 February 1922. He then joined the Young Revolutionary Movement.

Bhagat Singh was fond of quoting from Punjabi literature. His favourite poet was Allama Iqbal from Sialkot. In 1923, he won an essay competition by the Punjab Hindi Sahitya Sammelan.

When Lala Rajpat Rai died in 1928, as a result of a Lahore lathi charge, Bhagat—who was an eyewitness—vowed to avenge his death. He joined Shivaram Rajguru,

Jai Gopal and Sukhdev Thapar in a plot to kill the British police chief. However, mistaking his identity, he shot deputy superintendent of police J.P. Saunders instead. He then cut off his long hair, shaved his beard and fled Lahore.

The next year, in response to the Defence of India Act that gave the police extra powers, Batukeshwar Dutt and he threw a bomb into the corridor of the Central Legislative Assembly. No one was hurt, but they were both arrested.

Later, when tried for the Saunders killing, Bhagat Singh made a case against British rule. In jail, he went on a sixty-three-day hunger strike to plead for better conditions for political prisoners. He got his way!

But on 23 March 1931, he was hanged in Lahore, along with Rajguru and Sukhdev. He has since been regarded as a shaheed, or martyr.

10 ✤ Big Moment at Lahore

It was in 1929 that Jawaharlal was thrust into the limelight at the Congress session held at Lahore.

In the early months, he arranged a tour of the United Provinces for Gandhi. Jawaharlal was amazed that between 25,000 to over a lakh of people gathered wherever he travelled. Since sound amplification systems then were rather basic, Jawaharlal realized that most of them were happy just to catch a glimpse of the Mahatma over an ocean of heads.

At this time, Gandhi was unhappy that Jawaharlal kept insisting on independence as the Congress goal. He wanted a more moderate path, one that would take longer to achieve.

Sounding almost angry, Gandhi declared at the 1928 Calcutta session of the Congress, 'You may take the name of independence on your lips as the Muslims utter the name of Allah or the pious Hindus utter the name of Krishna or Rama, but all that muttering will be an empty formula if there is no honour behind it. If you are not prepared to stand by your words, where will independence be? Independence is a thing made of sterner stuff. It is not made by the juggling of words . . .'

Thousands of party members wondered who would take over as president of the Congress from Motilal, who had chaired the Calcutta session in 1928. Nominations for the post flew in from the party's committees across India. Gandhi, by far the most popular, declined to head the gathering. Of the other choices—Vallabhbhai Patel and Jawaharlal—he chose the younger Nehru.

Jawaharlal was just forty, and had been at loggerheads with his father very often in the recent past over how India was to win freedom. It was rare then in politics for a father to hand over the baton to his son in the country's main political party. Later, of course, Indira Gandhi led the nation, as did her son Rajiv Gandhi, though both were to die at the hands of assassins. Yet, even after a major argument between the son and the father, Motilal had earlier told a friend, 'The one thing I am proudest of is that I am Jawaharlal's father.'

What of Gandhi? He asked Jawaharlal if he felt strong enough to lead the Congress in case he was nominated, to which the younger man said he was capable of bearing the weight of the responsibility. Gandhi later wrote, 'This appointment of Jawaharlal Nehru as the captain is proof of the trust the nation reposes in its youth. Jawaharlal alone can do little. The youth of the country must be his arms and his eyes. Let them prove worthy of the trust.'

Meanwhile, two years after the Simon Commission came to India, the British introduced a different approach by making Lord Irwin the Viceroy in 1926. He was a calm and courteous man, who was determined not to provoke the people he ruled over on behalf of Her Majesty, Queen Victoria.

'We are in India to keep our tempers,' Lord Irwin told one of his assistants, who had a harder line in mind. On behalf of the British government, he offered India dominion status. That meant that the country could be a self-governing member state within the British Empire. Warring groups in the Congress saw this offer with different eyes, and agreed to meet this hand reaching out to them. But this was only if India was granted dominion status at a round table conference in London, and if all political prisoners were set free. Those were their pre-conditions. Though Jawaharlal was unhappy about the fact that the party no longer saw swaraj as its immediate goal, he signed the resolution. Then, he went to Gandhi to talk about his fears.

In a letter of November 1929, Gandhi tried to calm Jawaharlal's fears, as he would his own son, 'How shall I console you? Hearing others describe your state, I said to myself, "Have I been guilty of putting undue pressure on you?" I have always believed you to be above undue pressure. I have always honoured your resistance. It has always been honourable. Acting under that belief, I pressed my suit. Let this incident be a lesson. Resist me always, when my suggestion does not appeal to your head or heart. I shall not love you the less for that resistance. But why are you dejected? I hope there is no fear of public opinion in you . . .'

Consoled thus, Jawaharlal decided not to withdraw as Congress president at Lahore. He arrived riding a white horse as crowds cheered. Over 30,000 delegates and spectators had gathered at the venue. The proudest among those watching was Motilal, who had never dreamt that his son would succeed him in a position that was the highest honour that India could bestow on anyone. Swaruprani, who showered flowers as Jawaharlal rode by, watched him with tender, moist eyes. He glanced at her for a long moment as their eyes met.

Jawaharlal was clear about what he wanted from the British when he spoke at Lahore: 'Independence for us means complete freedom from British domination and British imperialism. Having attained our freedom, I have no doubt that India will welcome all attempts at world cooperation and federation and will even agree to give up part of her independence to a larger group of which she is an equal member.'

He also shared his mind on how he regarded non-violence, 'We have not the material or the training for organized violence, and individual or sporadic violence is a confession of despair. The great majority of us, I take it, judge the issue not on moral but on practical grounds and if we reject the way of violence, it is because it promises no substantial results. Any great movement for liberation must necessarily be a mass movement, and a mass movement must essentially be peaceful, except in times of organized revolt.'

At Lahore, the Congress gave a call for purna swaraj or complete independence. Even Gandhi agreed with this. Two hours past midnight, on 31 December 1929, thousands on the banks of the river Ravi cheered as the party passed the resolution.

On a chill dawn, Jawaharlal unfurled the tricolour flag with a charkha at its heart. It went up as the sun began to shine, and over 30,000 voices joined in the cry of *Inquilab zindabad* (long live the revolution).

Two days later, the party decided that 26 January was to be fixed as Independence Day (later changed to Republic Day). In 1930, huge crowds took a pledge with earnestness. It read:

We believe that it is the inalienable right of the Indian people, as of any other people, to have freedom and to enjoy the fruits of their toil and have the necessities of life, so that they have full opportunities of growth. We believe also that if any government deprives a people of these rights and oppresses them, the people have a further right to alter it or to abolish it.

Perhaps the party and the country took their cue from Jawaharlal's final words to the Lahore Congress session: *Success often comes to those who dare and act; it seldom goes to the timid who are ever afraid of the consequences. We play for high stakes; and if we seek to achieve great things it can only be through great dangers.*

26 January

26 January has been celebrated as Republic Day in India since 1950, when the country adopted its own constitution. The nation achieved independence on 15 August 1947, but its laws were based on the modified British Government of India Act 1935 until this event. The constitution was drafted by a committee chaired by Dr B.R. Ambedkar.

This day marks when India stopped being a British dominion, and became a republic instead. Dr Rajendra Prasad was then elected the first President of the sovereign state, taking over from C. Rajagopalachari or Rajaji, who had been India's first governor-general from June 1948 to January 1950.

26 January was declared India's 'Independence Day' by Mahatma Gandhi when the Congress adopted the purna swaraj declaration at its Lahore session in 1930. The party continued to celebrate it thus until 1950. The signing of the constitution on the same day respects the wishes of thousands of Indian freedom fighters, who wanted the date to mark total freedom from the Raj.

11 🪶 The Salt March

Jawaharlal may not have dreamt that the nation would regard him as a hero. But he soon realized that the masses loved him. People made up songs about him. He became a public legend. The common man even showered him with titles such as Bharat Bhushan (jewel of India) and Tyagamurti (embodiment of sacrifice).

His family found such praise reason enough to tease Jawaharlal, even at the dining table. He would chuckle as his sisters teasingly said, 'O Jewel of India, pass me the butter.' On occasion, even little Indira said, 'O Tyagamurti, what is the time now?'

Infected by the spirit of sacrifice and defiance in the country, Motilal decided to hand over their home Anand Bhawan to the nation. It was renamed Swaraj Bhawan (abode of independence). The house across the road that the family shifted to was now called Anand Bhawan.

It was at this point, in early 1930, that Gandhi decided to make the British tax on salt the target of his call for civil disobedience across India. He wrote, 'There is no article like salt, outside water, by touching which the state can touch the starving millions, the sick, the maimed, and the utterly helpless. The tax constitutes therefore the most inhuman poll tax the ingenuity of man can devise.'

He called on ordinary Indians to break the salt law, to make their own salt all along the country's coastline.

On 12 March, Gandhi, then sixty-one, set off from the Sabarmati ashram in Gujarat. Along with seventy followers to begin with, he began to walk to the small village of Dandi, about 388 km away. He stopped to talk to crowds that had gathered along the way. Often, more and more people joined the march, inspired by the Mahatma (great soul), a title by which the poet Rabindranath Tagore first referred to Gandhi in 1915.

Jawaharlal and Motilal met Gandhi at Jambusar, about halfway through the march. They were en route to Allahabad from a Congress meeting at Ahmedabad. Jawaharlal recalls in writing, 'That was my last glimpse of him then as I saw him, marching along at the head of his followers with firm step and a peaceful but undaunted look. It was a moving sight.'

So moved was Jawaharlal by what he saw and heard during the few hours they spent with Gandhi that he sent out this stirring message to the young in India:

The pilgrim marches onward. The field of battle lies before you, the flag of India beckons you, and freedom herself awaits your coming. Do you hesitate now, you who were so loudly on her side? Will you be mere lookers-on in this glorious struggle and see your best and bravest face the might of a great empire which has crushed your country and her children? Who lives if India dies? Who dies if India lives?

From a distance, Jawaharlal listened as Gandhi preached the message of non-violence every step of the way. 'If we are to stand the final heat of the battle,' Gandhi said to those who marched shoulder to shoulder with him, 'we must learn to stand our ground in the face of cavalry or baton charges and allow ourselves to be trampled under the horse's hooves or bruised in the charges.'

On 5 April, Gandhi reached Dandi. He had already told others that, if he was arrested, the elderly Abbas Tyabji was to lead them on. If Tyabji was also thrown behind bars, the poet-activist Sarojini Naidu was to take over.

Gandhi said his prayers in the morning. Then, along with thousands of others, he marched to the beach. Calmly, yet defiantly, he picked up a lump of crude salt. He had broken the British law. All around India, thousands of others took their cue from Gandhi. They marched to the beaches and picked up salt, without paying any tax.

Jawaharlal also led a vast procession that broke the law. He was arrested on 14 April 1930, as he was about to board a train from Allahabad to Raipur in the then Central Provinces. He was put behind bars at Naini Central Prison in the United Provinces. He was held there till 26 January 1931, with just eight days in between as a free man.

This time he was jailed alone in a space that was about 30.5 metres in diameter, surrounded by a 4.5 metre high wall. He stayed in one of the four cells at its centre, using another as his toilet and bathing space. Among the prisoners, this space was referred to as the *kuttaghar* or doghouse.

It was very hot indoors throughout summer. Often, he slept in the narrow corridor between the building and the wall, on a bed chained to the ground. Did the British imagine he would use it as a ladder to freedom? Whenever he was awakened by the jangling keys of the jailers, Jawaharlal would look up at the Pole Star, which remained steady in the night sky.

He was usually ready to face the new day as early as 3 a.m. or 4 a.m. During the day, he would spin cotton on his own charkha, then weave cloth for a few hours. Though no newspapers came his way, he was allowed to read a Hindi weekly with reports of the political movement. He learnt that over a lakh of people were rounded up during the protests. At places like Sholapur (now in Maharashtra), military rule was imposed. Those who carried the national flag were given prison terms of up to ten years!

In jail, the sunset hour was greeted with loud cries of *Gandhiji ki jai*. The cheer resounded across India in jails that held 9,000 prisoners or more.

After a lonely month in his cell, Jawaharlal was joined by Narmada Prasad Singh, also a political protester.

Motilal, though ailing already, took over the reins of the Congress. Gandhi was arrested on 5 May. With two popular leaders in custody, the common Indian could take it no more. They stopped entry to shops that sold foreign cloth. They refused to buy anything from booths selling imported liquor.

Among those who took part in these protests were Swaruprani and Kamala Nehru, along with Jawaharlal's sisters. He was surprised by the energy the frail Kamala put into her protests, at the way she organized support against the British throughout their city. Later, he would praise her in these words, 'She made up for inexperience by her fire and energy. Within a few months, she became the pride of Allahabad.'

On 30 June, Motilal joined Jawaharlal in jail, following his arrest at dawn. Both father and son cheered up at seeing each other again. Over the next month or so, the British government geared up towards the Round Table Conference in London, anxious that everyone should agree, to some extent, about the future of India.

This proved difficult to do because Gandhi was at the Yerawada jail near Poona, while the Nehrus were still at Naini. They asked Lord Irwin if they could consult each other, face to face, before the Congress could come to a decision. The Viceroy agreed that the Nehru duo could meet the Mahatma at Yerawada. He allowed Congress secretary Dr Syed Mahmud, also at Naini jail, to accompany them. But he said the other two members of the party working committee—Vallabhbhai Patel and Maulana Abul Kalam Azad—could not be part of the meeting because they were outside prison.

On 10 August 1930, a special train took Jawaharlal and Motilal to the Kirkee station near Poona. Huge crowds of people waved to them along the route. They reached late the next night, and were then detained in prison barracks for about twenty-four hours. After much debate, they were allowed to meet Gandhi alone at Yerawada. But the conditions they laid down as a group did not make the government happy.

As the Nehrus returned to Naini aboard another train on 16 August, even larger crowds stood by the tracks, cheering them on. They raised slogans, asking for an independent India.

Jawaharlal, meanwhile, sensed that his father was unwell. Though he sometimes asked for fine food, as he had during the better days in Anand Bhawan, Motilal seemed to tire easily. Besides, he seldom even disagreed with his son, which seemed unusual.

Back at Naini, Motilal was set free after just ten weeks in jail. Ranjit Pandit, Vijayalakshmi's husband, soon joined Jawaharlal behind bars. On 11 October, even Jawaharlal was set free at the end of his six-month sentence.

Once free, Jawaharlal rushed to the hill station of Mussoorie with Kamala on 13 October, to be with his ailing father. Four days later, Jawaharlal set out to address a large peasant conference at Allahabad. Along the way, he was stopped thrice. Each time, he was handed an official order stopping him from speaking in public. But he disobeyed them, asking over 2,000 peasants not to pay their taxes, as others had done at Bardoli.

As he drove to Anand Bhawan later, the police stopped his car and took him away to Naini prison once more. Kamala had to give this heart-breaking news to an ailing Motilal. Upset at his own frailty, Motilal called on Indians to celebrate Jawaharlal's birthday on 14 November in an unusual way—by reading aloud in public from his son's speech that had led to his arrest again. The response was enthusiastic across India. Over 5,000 people were held that day for joining in this unusual protest. Recalling that day in jail, Jawaharlal wrote, 'It was a unique birthday celebration.'

But as the no-tax campaign spread through the United Provinces, more and more ordinary prisoners were treated brutally. Aghast at this, Jawaharlal and his cellmates went on a three-day hunger strike.

Worried, Motilal hurried to see his son at Naini. This time, Jawaharlal was shocked to see his father much frailer than before. He pleaded with Motilal to shift to Calcutta for treatment and a long overdue rest. Motilal's health went into decline from this point onwards.

On 1 January 1931, Kamala joined Jawaharlal behind bars as she had been arrested, too. Asked if she had a message for the world outside, the usually shy woman said, 'I am happy beyond measure and proud to follow in the footsteps of my husband. I hope the people will keep the flag flying.'

By 26 January, Lord Irwin ordered that Jawaharlal and Gandhi should be set free without preconditions. Worried about Motilal, Jawaharlal rushed to Anand Bhawan. He held his father close in a long, gentle hug, knowing that the end was near this time.

Gandhi, too, rushed from Poona to Allahabad. As the two old friends held hands, Motilal whispered, 'I am going soon, Mahatmaji, and I shall not be here to see swaraj. But I know you have won it and will soon have it.'

At dawn on 6 February, the family and the doctors at a Lucknow hospital found that Motilal's face seemed unusually peaceful. Swaruprani was the first to realize that he was no more.

They draped his body in the Indian tricolour. With Jawaharlal by his side, they drove back to Anand Bhawan in Allahabad. All along the route, thousands of people stood quietly by. That night, after sunset, Motilal was cremated. Jawaharlal said a final farewell to his father.

He suddenly missed Motilal more deeply than he had ever thought possible. When Jawaharlal returned home from the funeral, he wrote, 'The stars were out and shining brightly when we returned lonely and desolate.'

With Motilal gone, Jawaharlal needed a guide he could trust as much as he did his father. With every passing day, he turned more and more to Gandhi.

Indira's growing years

Indira Nehru was aware of politics from the time she was a little girl in Allahabad. At four, she sat on her grandfather Motilal's lap in court, when her father and he were first tried, then sentenced, in December 1921.

At thirteen, Indira founded a children's political organization, the Vanar Sena or monkey army, named after events in the Ramayana. She and her young comrades organized rallies and flag marches, gave speeches and sang patriotic songs. On occasion, they did more important jobs, too, such as circulating banned Congress documents to its supporters. Once, while the police kept close watch on Anand Bhawan, Jawaharlal needed to get an important document to the local Congress office. Indira put the papers into her schoolbag and got it safely to them!

In October 1930, when Jawaharlal and Kamala visited the ailing Motilal in Mussoorie, Indira and her younger cousins, Vijayalakshmi Pandit's daughters, played at doing politics. Rita, the youngest child, would carry a national flag held proudly in front as they marched around the house, singing, '*Jhanda ooncha rahe hamara*' (keep our flag flying high).

In 1923, Indira joined St. Cecilia's, a private school in Allahabad. Three years later, while on a trip to Switzerland with her parents, she was admitted to L'Ecole Nouvelle. On her return to India in December 1927, she attended St. Mary's Convent in Allahabad. From May 1931 to April 1934, Indira was at Jahangir Vakil's Pupil's School in Poona, from where she graduated. Later, she spent a year at Rabindranath Tagore's Viswabharati University in Shantiniketan, where she was enchanted by the Nobel laureate's personality and his world view.

Once Kamala passed away in 1936, Jawaharlal took Indira to England. She studied at the Badminton School in Bristol. Two years later, she joined Somerville College, Oxford. In 1938, she returned to India and joined the Congress.

Indira was deeply affected by the Mahatma's ways. He was a frequent visitor to Anand Bhawan. Her first visit to his Sabarmati ashram was when both Motilal and Jawaharlal were in jail. Inspired by him, she joined the Quit India movement and spent about eight months in Naini jail. In 1947, she spent months working to provide relief to those stricken by the terrible riots and Partition.

12 ✒ In Step with Gandhi

Motilal had watched his son struggle with Gandhi's ideas of non-violence, satyagraha and swaraj. His own ideas of how to fight a battle that was legally right were quite different. He had seen Jawaharlal weigh up the difficult Gandhian way against the more easy-going lifestyle he had been brought up with. Perhaps it made Jawaharlal's choice easier when Motilal threw in his lot with the Mahatma, as did millions of their countrymen.

Though they did not agree about every political move that led to independence in August 1947, in some ways Jawaharlal came to regard Gandhi as a father figure of sorts.

At Anand Bhawan, after his father's death, Jawaharlal drew close to Kamala. She had proved she was as brave and as spirited as he was when she took to the streets in the struggle for independence. Jawaharlal and Kamala were to be together only for another five years before her death. In those years, he would be in prison again and again, while she was critically ill.

Meanwhile, the British were keen that Gandhi and other Congress leaders should attend the Round Table Conference in London to pave the way for the future. The Congress had stayed away from the conference's first session on 12 November 1930. Those who attended included Indian princes, Hindu Mahasabha leaders, Sikh and Muslim spokespersons and others.

Before its second session, from September to December 1931, some of those who attended the earlier conference tried to persuade Gandhi to join them. They asked him to talk to Lord Irwin about what he had in mind for India. Irwin agreed to meet Gandhi on 17 February 1931.

Jawaharlal did not agree with this. Why, he asked, would Gandhi agree to meet the enemy? 'As a satyagrahi, I must welcome above all a meeting with those who disagree with me,' said the Mahatma.

The future Prime Minister argued some more. 'I can understand your dealing with individuals in this way on personal or minor matters. But here you are up against an impersonal machine, the British Government.' Gandhi asked him to wait and watch for a while longer.

When Gandhi met Lord Irwin, he asked the Viceroy to be fair about some of the Congress demands. These included a pardon for all those in jail for their politics, a look at police brutality against protesters, the freedom to protest outside shops that sold foreign cloth or liquor, and the right to make salt.

Jawaharlal was puzzled. He wondered what the salt laws or the right to picket shops had to do with Indian independence. Could he trust Gandhi to win freedom for India?

Others in the Congress working committee shared Jawaharlal's unhappiness. They were aghast when Gandhi returned from a meeting with Irwin on 5 March, with a paper that agreed to Indian self-government with certain conditions. Jawaharlal was shocked that Gandhi had settled for less than complete independence.

Upset at being let down, Jawaharlal wept. Like Motilal, Gandhi tried to calm him down during a morning walk, assuring Jawaharlal that nothing was lost. But Jawaharlal did not give in so easily. 'What frightens me is your way of springing surprises upon us,' he replied. 'Although I have known you for fourteen years, there is something unknown about you which I cannot understand.'

The Gandhi–Irwin pact was signed on 5 March 1931. Like the satyagrahi he was, Gandhi felt neither the Congress nor the British had won a victory. On 27 August, Gandhi set sail from Bombay on a ship, *Rajputana*, for the Round Table Conference. 'I go to London with God as my only guide,' he told Jawaharlal as he left. Jawaharlal waved from the pier until the Mahatma's ship was a mere speck on the horizon. He did not meet his mentor for the next two years. When Gandhi returned, Jawaharlal was in prison again. Very little had been achieved at the London conference towards an independent India.

In the meantime, Jawaharlal had been busy. He tried to help peasants in the United Provinces, who did not have enough to pay land taxes. He heard of how the voices of Hindus and Muslims clashed at the Round Table Conferences in London in 1932. That made him extremely sad.

Meanwhile, younger Indians seemed to be losing

their patience with the Congress and Gandhi. In 1930, some youth armed with pistols and other arms took over a British armoury in Chittagong (which is now in Bangladesh). In Calcutta, a European was killed because his attackers thought he was the British superintendent of police! Such incidents hurt Gandhi deeply, but there seemed to be little he could do to stop rash young men on the warpath.

The British, angered by such rebellion, banned people from riding bicycles. Villages suspected of sheltering terrorists were fined heavily. Political activists had to stay at home for weeks.

Jawaharlal tried to talk angry Indians out of this means of protest. After a meeting in Calcutta in November 1931, he was leaving for the station. En route, he met two terrorists who were barely twenty. Their eyes blazing with fury, they told him, 'We have come to warn you. Your propaganda against terrorism is harming the country. It is keeping the young men away from us . . . If you continue your criticism, we shall deal with you as we have done with some others.'

In Allahabad, Kamala was ill again. Jawaharlal took her to Bombay for treatment, then set out for Karnataka. When he was about to step off a train on his return to Allahabad, he received an order that would confine him to the city of his birth. But this was addressed to 'Jawahir Lal'. Cross about this, he shot off a letter to the magistrate.

On his way to Bombay to see Kamala again, he was arrested at the small station of Iradatganj. On 26 December 1931, he found himself back in Naini jail.

During his trial in January 1932, he received two years of sentence because the magistrate was upset about his letter.

Once again, the British had given themselves the power to arrest and hold people as prisoners of the state. Soon, Gandhi and Vallabhbhai Patel were behind bars, too. By 10 January 1932, the Congress was banned. Within four months, 80,000 people were sent to jail. With the rounding up of so many men, women took to the streets in protest. Nehru's sisters Vijayalakshmi and Krishna were also put in jail.

In April 1932, his mother Swaruprani sat in a chair at the head of a procession in Allahabad. During a police lathi charge, she was knocked off her chair, and beaten further. A police officer, who found her lying by the wayside, drove her back to Anand Bhawan. Hearing false reports of her death, crowds attacked the police. Many innocent people died in the firing that ensued.

Jawaharlal read about these events only a few days later. Distressed, he wrote, 'The thought of my frail old mother lying bleeding on the dusty road obsessed me. I wondered how I would have behaved if I had been there.' A month later, Swaruprani visited her son in jail at Bareilly, where he had been shifted to. She wore the bandages on her head, almost like a badge of courage.

As civil disobedience continued, though at a slower pace, Jawaharlal often thought of the peasants in his province. This was especially so when rumours reached him about the government taking over Anand Bhawan.

He imagined his mother being turned out of their home, and the British flag fluttering over it, instead of the tricolour. He thought that losing his family home might bring him closer to those in Indian villages. Much of this proved to be untrue, but the British did take over and sell his car.

Jawaharlal's attention soon shifted to Gandhi yet again. The Mahatma had decided to fight for the rights of those he called the Harijans, then known as the untouchables (now the Dalits).

It was in protest against the third Round Table Conference decision to give these people a separate electorate that Gandhi decided to fast unto death on 20 September 1932. Nehru was upset by this. He was troubled by the prospect of losing his mentor and father figure. It was probably the first time in history that such a fast had been used as a political weapon.

Six days later, when the British conceded his demands, Gandhi called off his fast. Relieved, Jawaharlal sent him a telegram from jail. It read, 'No sacrifice too great for suppressed downtrodden classes. Freedom must be judged by freedom of lowest but feel danger of other issues obscuring only goal. Am unable to judge from religious viewpoint. Danger your methods being exploited by others, but how can I presume to advise a magician? Love ...'

All around India, political activity was stepped up. In March 1933, the banned Congress tried to hold its annual session at Calcutta. Thousands of delegates were held on their way there. They included the fragile

Swaruprani, who was arrested at Asansol, then detained for a few days. Despite lathi charges, a thousand others did gather to pass some resolutions.

Disturbed by the violence that erupted during the civil disobedience movement, Gandhi decided on a twenty-one-day fast from 8 May 1933, to purify himself. During the eighteen months of the movement, nearly 1,00,000 people had gone to jail. Instead, the Mahatma now called for individuals who would offer satyagraha or civil disobedience as opposed to mass action.

Jawaharlal, who was not sure if he supported Gandhi's decisions, was released from jail twelve days before his term was to end. He rushed to the side of Swaruprani, who was in hospital.

Between 26 December 1931 and 4 September 1935, Jawaharlal was a free man for just about nine months. Already in his mid-forties, he spent time each day doing yoga. His favourite pose was the shirshasana, during which he stood on his head, supported by his interlocked fingers, his elbows on the floor.

'It's a complete reversal of the normal situation. The body is forced to adapt itself to new conditions. One sits or walks about all day and forgets to give the spine a change,' Jawaharlal once told an American journalist.

In jail, often alone, Jawaharlal had conversations with pigeons at Bareilly or watched the antics of the parrots that abounded at Naini. At Dehradun, he would tune in to the cry of the koel, or delight in the gliding kites and eagles overhead. At Bareilly, he was upset when a baby monkey captured by other prisoners was tied to a post by a string. It cried aloud night and day. Soon, a huge monkey lowered itself into the yard, pushed aside the threatening sticks that came its way and took the little one away to safety. That made Jawaharlal smile.

Sometimes, he would allow a baby squirrel to scamper up his leg, even rest on his knee for a minute or two. In Dehradun, he adopted a stray dog, which later had a litter of puppies. He once nursed a sick puppy through the night.

Maybe because he was not free to walk in the world outside the prison walls, Jawaharlal read widely. Some of his favourite books included those by long-ago visitors to India such as the Chinese traveller Hiuen Tsang in the 7th century, Marco Polo from Italy, and Ibn-Batuta, the 14th century Moroccan scholar-traveller.

He constantly worried about the three women in his life—his mother, his wife and his teenaged daughter. On her thirteenth birthday, he began a series of letters from prison to Indira Priyadarshini, which were later published as *Glimpses of World History*. The first letter was written on 26 October 1930, the last on 9 August 1933.

The opening words of that first letter to Indira read:

On your birthday, you have been in the habit of receiving presents and good wishes. Good wishes you will still have in full measure, but what present can I give you from Naini prison? My presents cannot be very material or solid. They can only be of the air and of the mind and spirit, such as a good fairy might have bestowed on you—something that even the high walls of prison cannot stop . . .

Once he was free, Jawaharlal met Gandhi for the first time in over two years. Soon, the Mahatma was to set out on a nine-month mission to uplift the downtrodden. He travelled by foot, by train, car or bullock cart over 20,117 km across India, raising about Rs 8,00,000 for the cause. Jawaharlal was impressed by the energy involved in this campaign to uplift the poor, though he did not entirely agree with the Mahatma, who seemed to have forgotten about swaraj for the moment.

On 15 January 1934, a terrible earthquake struck Bihar. It destroyed over a million homes in towns and villages, across 77,700 sq km, affecting over 10,000,000 people. On his way back from Calcutta for Kamala's medical treatment, and a visit to Shantiniketan, Jawaharlal got involved in relief and aid work for the victims. At Monghyr, he picked up a spade and shovel. He began to dig through the rubble, to help to distribute aid, even to raise funds for the poor in distress. He did this for days on end.

Back at Anand Bhawan, Jawaharlal looked and felt more tired than ever before in his life. But before the second day was over, he was under arrest again because of the speeches he had made in Calcutta. As he was whisked away in the police car, Kamala fainted. Did she know by intuition that they did not have much time left together?

She left for treatment at Badenweiler in Germany in May 1935, though Jawaharlal was still in Almora jail. In September, he flew for five days from Allahabad through Karachi, Baghdad, and Cairo to reach Kamala. He thought how, on one occasion, a friend had got her a blanket to ward off the bitter cold as she led a protest in Allahabad in 1930. When this friend returned, she found Kamala shivering in her thin sari. The blanket warmed an elderly lady who sat by her side!

Later, the couple travelled from Germany to London when Kamala felt a little better. It was there that Jawaharlal learnt he had been elected Congress president again for its April 1936 session. Was it time to return home? Should he give up on politics?

Kamala was quite clear about the path her husband had to take. 'You must go. There is no question of your resigning. After April, you can come back to me,' she said.

But on 28 February 1936, Kamala breathed her last, as Indira and Jawaharlal stood by her bedside.

Flying back, Jawaharlal sent a telegram to his publishers in London. He wanted to thus dedicate his autobiography, which he had written in prison: 'To Kamala who is no more.'

Before he left Europe, Jawaharlal could feel the stirrings of a great war in the making. What role would India play in this?

Yoga every morning

Jawaharlal often worried about the frail health of others in his family. In the 1920s, he decided that he had to keep fit, both physically and mentally.

While in jail or on the long march to free India, it was impossible to swim or play cricket or tennis to keep fit. So, he chose to do hatha yoga. This is a system first put together by a 15th century sage, Yogi Swatmarama. Hatha yoga is made up of physical exercises that the ancient yogis or sages used as they prepared for deep, silent meditation.

One of Jawaharlal's yoga teachers was Dhirendra Brahmachari, who later taught Indira Gandhi. As Jawaharlal went through the *asanas* or postures of the Surya Namaskar each morning, he felt a quickened heartbeat as his spine flexed. Energy flowed through him as if the sun had touched each cell.

13 🖋 World War II, Then Partition

Jawaharlal returned home to India in March 1936. All around Europe, he had seen the shadow of the Nazi swastika grow, as jackboots threatened to trample over weaker countries. In the east, Japan was gearing up to attack China again. He agonized over what decision India should take if Britain joined the war in Europe. Could India make its own voice heard above that of the British Raj?

Addressing the Congress session at Lucknow in April 1936, Jawaharlal wondered why the once active party now seemed to lack energy. Its membership had dropped drastically to below half a million people. He was keen that the party should contest the elections in the coming year, but not take office to protest against British rule. Many others in the party, including Vallabhbhai Patel, did not agree with him.

Between April 1936 and February 1937, he spent over 130 days on the election trail. Jawaharlal travelled more than 1,46,073 km across India by plane and train, car and lorry, horse and bullock-drawn carts, steamers and paddle boats, canoes, bicycles and horses, camels and elephants. He even trekked through dozens of villages on foot.

Often working about twenty hours a day, he would address up to twelve meetings. Some were attended by a thousand people, some by over 1,00,000. The over 2,00,00,000 possible voters he spoke to included farmers and factory workers, traders and students, lawyers and doctors, even those who cleaned out public toilets.

In a Punjab village, he came across about a thousand voices shouting, *Bharat Mata ki jai!* Jawaharlal asked who they were cheering for. They were taken aback. They went silent. Gently, Jawaharlal explained that they were all children of Mother India or Bharat Mata. 'Who are these sons and daughters? They are you, all of you, and I. So, when you cry *jai,* you are shouting your own *jai* as well as the *jai* of all our brothers and sisters throughout Hindustan. Remember this,' he added.

Soon, the Congress found itself facing another major hurdle: the Muslim League, founded by Mohammed Ali Jinnah. Though this party did not fare well at the elections, Jinnah kept insisting that it was the voice of all the Muslims in India. Eventually, this would lead to the Partition of India, and the bloodbath that followed, dividing millions of families forever.

When the poll results came out in 1937, the Congress controlled eight of India's eleven provinces. It had won 715 out of the 1,585 seats. However, Jawaharlal was upset when the Congress chose to form ministries in six provinces, without achieving all they had set out to do. But they arrived at some goals. They eased the debt of villagers. They introduced basic education. These ministries remained in office till November 1939.

What happened then? The Congress withdrew from the British-led government because the rulers had chosen to commit India to World War II without asking any of its elected representatives.

By the summer of 1936, the Italian dictator Mussolini and Hitler had joined hands to form the Rome–Berlin Axis in Europe. Defying the League of Nations, Japan seized Nanking and much of the Yangtse area in China in 1937. Next, it joined hands with the Axis powers. By March 1938, Hitler seized Austria, then Czechoslovakia. The nightmare of World War II had begun in Europe.

Though it knew that he hated Nazi policies, the German government invited Jawaharlal on an official visit that year. Instead, he chose to go to Spain and Czechoslovakia, with a short stay in Britain. In a letter to the *Manchester Guardian* in September 1938, he wrote, 'The people of India have no intention of submitting to any foreign decision on war . . . If Britain is on the side of democracy, then its first task is to eliminate empire from India. That is the sequence of events in Indian eyes, and to that sequence the people of India will adhere.'

It was while on a visit to China in 1939 that Jawaharlal heard that Hitler had invaded Poland on 1 September. Once back home, he found that Lord Linlithgow, as Viceroy, had announced that India was at war with the Axis powers. He added that the British were fighting for democracy and freedom. Angered, Jawaharlal and millions of Indians asked, 'Whose freedom?' Lord Linlithgow, in response, decided to invite some Indians to be a part of his war council. But he paid no heed to the Congress call from Delhi for a free India. Gandhi did not approve of the British move.

On 17 October 1940, Vinoba Bhave delivered an anti-war speech at Wardha, got arrested, and sent to prison. Over the next year, 30,000 men and women were jailed for the same offence.

At Anand Bhawan, Jawaharlal was to face another personal tragedy. Swaruprani fell to a third stroke of paralysis, as her children sat by her bedside in 1938. It was her love for Jawaharlal that kept her going through all the tough times in her life.

Jawaharlal, meanwhile, found himself back in jail from October 1940 to December 1941, then a last term from August 1942 to June 1945. During the freedom struggle, Jawaharlal spent over nine years in jail. It was in December 1921 that the British Raj first sent him to jail. He was imprisoned eight more times afterwards.

Tried at Gorakhpur in 1940 for his speeches to peasants there, Jawaharlal said to the British magistrate:

Individuals count for little; they come and go, as I shall go when my time is up. Seven times I have been tried and convicted by British authority in India, and many years of my life lie buried within prison walls. An eighth time or a ninth, or a few more years, make little difference.

But it is no small matter what happens to India and her millions of sons and daughters. That is the issue before me, and that ultimately is the issue before you, sir. If the British government imagines it can continue to exploit them and play about with them against their

> *will, as it has done for so long in the past, then it is grievously mistaken. It has misjudged their present temper and read history in vain.*

On the war front, in 1941, the Germans took over Yugoslavia and Greece. Mussolini lost the lands he had conquered in north Africa. The British took over Somaliland, then Ethiopia, from the Axis forces. Then, the German general Erwin Rommel reclaimed Libya. To the east, the Japanese forces came up to the Indo-Burma border.

On 9 August 1942, the Congress gathering in Bombay sent out a clear message to the British: 'Quit India'.

Arrested yet again, Gandhi said, 'Let every non-violent soldier of freedom write out the slogan *Do or Die* on a piece of paper or cloth, and pin it on his clothes, so that in case he died in the course of offering satyagraha, he might be distinguished by that sign from other elements who do not subscribe to non-violence.'

Gandhi was taken away to the Aga Khan's residence at Poona. Jawaharlal and other Congress leaders were held at Ahmednagar fort, about 322 km from Bombay. At the latter military station, the prisoners, aged between forty-four and sixty-eight, were housed in small rooms around a quadrangle of straggly grass. They spent hours reading, talking politics, playing games and tending this patch of green. Jawaharlal, his companions recall, would fry eggs for all of them. Or explain how to toast bread perfectly or boil water for tea!

Another project came to occupy Jawaharlal's waking hours at Ahmednagar. On 13 April 1944, he began to write a book, *The Discovery of India*, which was ready in about five months. It covers India's history from prehistoric times to British rule, discusses Indian classics like the Mahabharata and the Vedas, and Indian traditions of art, science and philosophy. Every word reveals Jawaharlal's love for his motherland.

Outside the jail walls, mobs across the country rose in response to the Quit India call. The British Government admitted that over 940 had died and 1,630 were injured in firing. Later, Jawaharlal estimated that over 10,000 had died, while 60,000 were arrested when the movement came to a close. Over 250 railway stations were damaged, 550 post offices attacked, seventy police stations burnt, and eighty-five other government buildings destroyed.

Instead of understanding the message that the Indian people were sending out, the British government decided to impose fines totalling Rs 90,00,000 on its starving villagers! Gandhi decided to go on a twenty-one-day fast in jail protesting against this, during February–March 1943, unless the government provided relief to the injured or starving Indians. He declined a British offer to set him free. Jawaharlal wrote about the Mahatma: 'Which way he might turn in a crisis it was difficult to say but whichever way it was, it would make a difference. He might go the wrong way according to our thinking, but it would always be a straight way.'

In the east of India, a terrible food crisis was underway. Lord Linlithgow as Viceroy had chosen to ignore that the Japanese march through Burma had cut off precious rice supplies to Bengal. By the time he left in 1943, after seven-odd years as Viceroy, the Great Bengal Famine had claimed over 35,00,000 lives.

All over Calcutta, people who had crawled there in search of food, lay dying on the streets. Enraged by the British indifference to such a tragedy, Jawaharlal said, 'Corpses cannot be easily overlooked. They come in the way.'

At Ahmednagar prison, Jawaharlal kept track of the raging war through newspapers. He read of how north Africa had been cleared of Axis forces in 1943. Of how Mussolini had lost his dictatorship. Of how the Russian army drove the Germans from their land in 1944. By May Day in 1945, the war in Europe was over!

To the east, he learnt of the slower Japanese advance, though they did cross Burma and come into Manipur. How would the British respond to this, he asked himself.

The British government, led by Prime Minister Winston Churchill, decided to make a special offer to the Indian people. He called for elections, promising India dominion status if all went well. The Viceroy's executive committee was to be reshaped, so that it would be all-Indian, apart from him and the Commander-in-Chief of the armed forces. Gandhi was already out of jail. Nehru was set free on 15 June 1945, after 1,041 days in jail.

But when Maulana Abul Kalam Azad, as Congress president, attended the meeting with Lord Wavell, the

Viceroy, he found all was not smooth sailing. For Jinnah was against the two Muslims nominated by the Congress. He insisted that only the Muslim League could nominate Muslims for the executive committee. By July 1945, Wavell called off the talks, fearing a breakdown.

Soon, American atom bombs fell on Hiroshima and Nagasaki. Japan surrendered on 15 August. World War II was over.

In late 1945, three officers—a Hindu, a Muslim and a Sikh—of the Indian National Army (INA) launched by Netaji Subhas Chandra Bose were put on trial at Delhi's Red Fort. Though convicted, the British released them soon afterwards. Jawaharlal donned his legal robes for the first time in thirty years to defend them.

Of the trial, he felt, 'It became a trial of strength between the will of the Indian people and the will of those who held power in India, and it was the will of the people that triumphed in the end.'

In the 1946 elections to the legislatures, the Congress won many seats. But the Muslim League captured nearly 75 per cent of the Muslim votes. India felt like a bonfire that needed a spark to light it.

In February, Indians serving in the Royal Navy proved to be the spark. In protest against their poor working conditions, they attacked British officers, hoisted the Indian tricolour, then shouted, *Quit India*, or *Jai Hind*. They even took over the British vice admiral's ship.

Was this the first sign of how India would reclaim its freedom? The British sent a three-man Cabinet Mission, led by Lord Pethick Lawrence, to discuss the transfer of power to Indian leaders. It ruled out the idea of Pakistan. The Viceroy announced that he would form an interim government that would include major political parties.

Jinnah, however, kept insisting that Wavell should agree to the formation of Pakistan. When the Viceroy disagreed, the Muslim League leader called for Direct Action. This was the opposite of all that Gandhi stood for.

On 16 August 1946, Muslims in Calcutta killed thousands of Hindus. The violence which followed over the next year and more led to massacres of innocent men, women and children in trains, and bloody riots. When India became independent after the Partition of Punjab and Bengal to create Pakistan, over 1,15,00,000 people had to leave behind their homes, often their families, to cross the border. They included Hindus, Muslims and Sikhs. A trail of blood followed in their wake. Some reports say over 2,00,000 people perished in the creation of Pakistan.

From Jawaharlal's pen

Jawaharlal, who was later known as a scholar or Pandit Nehru, loved to read and write. These are the books that he wrote in his lifetime:

- *The Discovery of India*
- *Glimpses of World History*
- *An Autobiography*
- *Letters from a Father to his Daughter*
- *The Story of the World*, a brief account of the story of the earth as told in letters to his daughter.

14 ✤ Freedom at Midnight

On 22 March 1947, Lord Louis Mountbatten arrived in India. He had an important job to do—to transfer political power to India by June 1948. Ninety years earlier, when India first came to be ruled by the British, Queen Victoria reigned in London. Lord Mountbatten, her great-grandson, was to be the last British Viceroy, and independent India's first governor-general.

At their very first meeting in Delhi, he said to Jawaharlal, 'Mr Nehru, I want you to regard me not as the last Viceroy winding up the British Raj but as the first to lead the way to the new India.'

In time, his friendship with Jawaharlal was to deepen. So was the bond between the first Prime Minister of independent India and Lady Mountbatten, who was a god-daughter of British King Edward VII. She was known for her selfless social service during India's Partition.

The Congress kept insisting that the British should set a date for their withdrawal. They were tired of secret plots and unclear plans. India had but months to go before independence. 'This simply cannot go on,' Nehru complained to Mountbatten one day as part of his executive council. 'You won't govern yourself, and you won't let us govern.'

After lying low for a short while, Jinnah began to insist once more that Pakistan should be made up of an undivided Bengal and Punjab, an idea that no one in the Congress would agree to. Nor would Gandhi, who was totally against the Partition. Nehru was aghast when, in May 1947, Jinnah demanded an 800 mile corridor through India to connect the two wings of Pakistan! Meanwhile, the 565 Indian princes and kings had to each decide whether to opt for India or Pakistan.

The Mahatma had decided to take a back seat for a while. Most Congress decisions during this time were taken by Jawaharlal and Vallabhbhai Patel.

The days that led to Indian independence were difficult. On 20 July 1947, there were riots and explosions in Lahore. Two days later, mob violence rocked Bharatpur in Rajasthan and Kharagpur in Bengal. Riots took place in Hyderabad, Aurangabad, Nagpur, Calcutta, Chandernagore, Amritsar and Lahore on 27 July. In Rawalpindi, about 1,00,000 people fled their homes. On 3 August, there were disturbances in Lahore, Hyderabad, Bombay and Sholapur. By 4 August, the refugee population in Delhi had reached 80,000. There was not enough food or shelter for all.

Disturbed by all the violence around him, the Mahatma chose to stay away from the centre of power, in a Muslim-dominated slum in Calcutta, appealing to people to maintain peace. In his evening prayer meeting on 14 August, he observed, 'We'll be free tomorrow but the country will split tonight.' In that city, Hindus and

Muslims hoisted India's national flag together, while rioting continued unabated in Punjab.

In Delhi, India's Constituent Assembly, set up to draft its first constitution, met on 9 December 1946. On 15 August 1947, it became independent India's first Parliament.

At midnight on 14 August 1947, Jawaharlal Nehru was three months short of fifty-eight. Dressed in a pale cream *achkan,* a pristine white khadi cap on his head, he rose to speak to the independent nation as its first Prime Minister.

On the streets of New Delhi, streams of light glittered from public buildings and from the homes of the rich. It was raining heavily, yet crowds thronged the street. Gaiety was in the air. In the villages across the subcontinent, over acres of wheat and rice, over hilltops and forest, bonfires marked the fact that the nation was awake.

In Parliament house, its red and white sandstone gleaming under moonlight, faces looked up at Jawaharlal with anticipation. Some sought hope of a new dawn, some seemed weary after the long struggle for freedom, some needed guidance on whether India had made the right choice.

As the clock struck midnight, Jawaharlal stood up to address them. His voice was carried to millions of Indians over the radio. The rose in his buttonhole had wilted slightly. His voice brimmed over with emotion. Though his eyes had shadows beneath them, they seemed to brighten as Jawaharlal began to speak:

Long years ago we made a tryst with destiny and now the time comes when we shall redeem our pledge, not wholly or in full measure, but very substantially. At the stroke of midnight, when the world sleeps, India will awake to life and freedom. A moment comes, which comes but rarely in history, when we step from the old to the new, when an age ends, when the soul of a nation, long suppressed, finds utterance. It is fitting that at this solemn moment we take a pledge of dedication to the service of India and her people and to the still larger cause of humanity . . .

. . . On this day, our first thoughts go to the architect of this freedom, the Father of our Nation, who, embodying the old spirit of India, held aloft the torch of freedom and lighted up the darkness that surrounded us. We have often been unworthy followers of his and have strayed from his message, but not only we, but the succeeding generations, will remember this message and bear the imprint in their hearts of this great son of India, magnificent in his faith and strength, courage and humility. We shall never allow the torch of freedom to be blown out, however high the wind or stormy the tempest . . .

. . . The service of India means the service of the millions who suffer. It means the ending of poverty and ignorance and disease and inequality of opportunity . . . The ambition of the greatest man of our generation has been to wipe the tear from every eye. That may be beyond

> *us, but so far as there are tears and suffering, so long our*
> *work will not be over . . .*
>
> *. . . To the people of India whose representatives we*
> *are, we make an appeal to join us with faith and confidence*
> *on this great adventure. This is no time for petty or*
> *destructive criticism, no time for ill-will or blaming others.*
> *We have to build the noble mansion of free India where*
> *all her children will dwell.*

On 15 August 1947, Sardar Patel, the man who shared in governing independent India in its early years, was seventy-two. Gandhi was seventy-eight. To both Jawaharlal and Patel, who were as different as can be, Gandhi was Bapu, a father figure they revered.

'He did not descend from the top,' Nehru once wrote of Bapu. 'He seemed to emerge from the millions of India.'

With Partition, over ten million human beings began their two-way march across Punjab, with another million moving to safety in Bengal, one of the largest mass migrations in human history. Anger and violence was in the air. In Bengal, trucks of corpses were left behind in neighbourhoods, provoking more killings in revenge. In Lahore and Delhi, trainloads of slaughtered families pulled in at stations. As thousands of families moved through Punjab, even nature seemed angry. The rivers in Punjab flooded their banks, drowning people in their refugee camps.

Saddened by the price that India had to pay for freedom, Gandhi left for Noakhali, which is now in southern Bangladesh, in November 1947. Hindu–Muslim riots had been raging there for weeks. East Pakistan became Bangladesh after a war in December 1971.

The Mahatma arrived in Noakhali clad in a khadi loincloth, another khadi cloth over his shoulder. He heard stories of how the landlords' homes had been looted, how people jumped into village fish ponds and hid under the water hyacinths to save their lives. He walked barefoot across narrow bridges. He stopped to ask people who came to his side, 'Have you thought of what caused this? I'm going to the interior. I'll find out what was the real cause, and then I'll be able to help.'

Angry Hindus and Sikhs attacked Muslim homes in Delhi in 1947, looting and killing, blind with hatred. Often, Jawaharlal would walk through a raging crowd, talking to them, reasoning with some, trying to calm them down. On occasion, he would succeed. He seemed to have no fear of death.

On 9 September, Jawaharlal spoke to the nation over radio:

> *I go to the countryside, and people with spikes and all sorts of destructive weapons, when they see me, shout, Mahatma Gandhi ki jai! Jawaharlal ji jai! I feel ashamed to hear these cries from these people, who might have committed murder, loot and arson, in the name of*

> *Mahatma Gandhi. It is not by shouting slogans that they will wash off the evil deeds that they have done. And even we will not get over these evil deeds by just honouring the Mahatma in name, and not following what he had told us all these long years . . .*

On 30 January 1948, just ten days after Gandhi had broken a fast in which he had called on all Hindus, Muslims and Sikhs to live like brothers, he was walking to an evening prayer meeting at Birla House in Delhi. Jawaharlal had fasted alongside Bapu, until the Mahatma had asked him to stop on 18 January. Once he did, a weak Gandhi had scribbled in a note, 'May you long remain Jawahar, the jewel of India.'

As Gandhi walked with his hands on the shoulders of Manu and Abha, his human 'walking sticks', a man named Nathuram Godse came up, with his hands folded in a namaste. Bowing, he shot the Mahatma point blank three times.

Jawaharlal, who heard the news of the assassination at his residence, rushed to Birla House. Clutching the hands of his Bapu, he wept uncontrollably. By his side stood Patel, India's Deputy Prime Minister, much more in control of his emotions. He and Jawaharlal had not agreed about many things since independence. Finding them together by Gandhi's body, Mountbatten said to the two, 'At my last interview with Gandhiji, he told me that his dearest wish was to bring about a full reconciliation between the two of you.' Jawaharlal hugged Patel, as if to seal that bond of brotherhood.

The night before the Mahatma's cortege moved to the cremation ground on the banks of the Yamuna, mourned by over 7,00,000 Indians, Jawaharlal made a radio speech. He said:

> *The light has gone out of our lives, and there is darkness everywhere . . . and yet I was wrong. For the light that shone in this country was no ordinary light. The light that has illumined this country for these many, many years will illumine this country for many more years, and a thousand years later, that light will still be seen in this country and the world will see it and it will give solace to innumerable hearts. For that light represented something more than the immediate present, it represented the living, the eternal truths, reminding us of the right path, drawing us from error, taking this ancient country to freedom.*

After the funeral, thousands went home with tears in their eyes, sadness in their hearts. The next morning, Jawaharlal went back to Rajghat, where Gandhi had been cremated. As he gently laid flowers on the remains of the Mahatma, he said, almost under his breath, 'Bapuji, here are flowers. Today, at least, I can offer them to your bones and ashes. Where shall I offer them tomorrow, and to whom?'

While mourning the Mahatma, Jawaharlal remembered the pathways Gandhi had trekked through India. He had loved the humblest of peasants, and been loved by the richest of landlords and industrialists. He knew the Indian soil from the Himalayas to Kanyakumari, from the paddy fields of Tamil Nadu to the tea gardens of Assam. He knew the burden of the downtrodden must be lifted if India was to prosper in the coming years. As Prime Minister of independent India, Jawaharlal was to try to speak like the Mahatma—of being without fear, of freedom from hate, of loving and forgiving.

Six years before his death, Gandhi had known this of his successor. Speaking to the Congress at Wardha, he said, 'Somebody has suggested that Jawaharlal and I are estranged. It will require much more than differences of opinion to estrange us. We have had differences from the moment we became co-workers, and yet I have said for some years and say now that not Rajaji (C. Rajagopalachari) but Jawaharlal will be my successor. He says that he does not understand my language, and that he speaks a language foreign to me. This may or may not be true. But language is no bar to a union of hearts. And I know this, that when I am gone he will speak my language.'

In his seventeen years as Indian Prime Minister, from 1947 to 1964, Jawaharlal tried hard to tread in the footsteps of the Mahatma. Sometimes he succeeded, at others he did not.

He did not imagine, then, that his daughter Indira

Gandhi would be Indian Prime Minister from January 1966 to March 1977, then from January 1980 to October 1984. Nor did he dream that her son, Rajiv Gandhi, would follow in her footsteps from October 1984 to December 1989. Or that Rajiv's widow, Sonia Gandhi, would lead the Congress Party today. That her son, Rahul Gandhi, would play an active role in the Congress win in the 2009 general elections.

15 August 1947

Hundreds of thousands of people in Delhi did not sleep that night. They realized they were part of history in the making. As the tricolour was unfurled over Parliament, there was a tremendous buzz both inside and outside the building.

In the afternoon, the route to the Kingsway Plaza was packed. People made their way in crammed buses, trucks, horse-drawn tongas and on foot to await Jawaharlal at the flagstand. In that jostling mass, Lord Mountbatten rescued a child in danger of being trampled underfoot. Women who fainted were brought to the flagstand to recover. Even the Prime Minister had to be rescued from the jostling crowd to raise the Indian flag.

Jawaharlal did so in a hurry, so that the crowd would ease. As the tricolour was unfurled, a rainbow emerged from the mass of monsoon clouds. Lord Mountbatten pointed it out. The crowd broke into spontaneous applause.

In the evening, Jawaharlal and Lord Mounbatten held a reception, where they shook hands with hundreds and hundreds of people.

In Bombay, the Gateway of India was lit brilliantly, so were the ships in the Arabian Sea harbour. In high spirits, Indians even danced atop trams and buses!

In the south, Madras seemed to be celebrating a hundred festivals, all at once. Every school, every college, every public building was ablaze with light. People came into the streets in their best clothes, as if they were going to a wedding. Renowned Carnatic classical musicians performed live at different locations throughout the day.

Midnight at Nagpur seemed like dawn because of the brilliant illumination in the streets. People embraced total strangers with delight. Others distributed sweets in the streets. Even the Pink City of Jaipur was dazzling, its sandstone buildings alight with flickering lamps, in ordinary homes and the magnificent City Palace alike.

Phillips Talbot, reporting for the *Chicago Daily* from India that day, recalls two amazing facts. That Hindus and Muslims in India embraced each other like brothers in the streets that day, and there seemed to be no animosity towards the stray foreigners in the street.

15 ✍ A Prime Minister is Born

From 15 August 1947 onwards, Jawaharlal found himself with more to do than seemed possible. In time, the world was to see him as a man with a dream for the Indian people, and deep ideas for peace in the world.

It took the Constituent Assembly four years to draft an Indian constitution. Its members were inspired by democracies such as the United States, Canada, Britain, France and Switzerland. The constitution made India a republic within the British Commonwealth from Republic Day or 26 January 1950.

In January 1952, India held its first general elections to the Lok Sabha. Every person over twenty-one was allowed a vote. It was the world's largest democratic election ever. Of the 17,66,00,000 people with the power to vote, about 16,00,00,000 cast their ballots. Over 4,400 representatives were chosen by ballot. They came from seventy-seven political parties. What was remarkable was that eighty per cent of the voters were illiterate. Other countries in Asia and Africa, which were afraid of elections because their people had not been to school, learnt lessons from India. The Congress won 364 of the 399 Lok Sabha seats.

In free India, the eighteen state-like units and 565 princely states had to be reorganized. By September 1955, a committee had come up with a formula for just sixteen states, with three areas under the Central Government.

By December 1950, even Sardar Patel was no more. Nehru found himself facing a host of problems, including the arrival of eight million refugees from Punjab and Bengal, who needed homes and livelihoods. Though troublesome, kingdoms like Junagadh in Gujarat and Hyderabad decided to throw in their lot with India.

But Kashmir was a different story. A state with borders along the then Soviet Union, China, Afghanistan and Pakistan, its people included Muslims and Hindus, besides Buddhists in Ladakh. Its maharaja took weeks to decide whether to join India or Pakistan. In September 1947, Pakistani tribesmen made their way into Kashmir. Its ruler pleaded for Indian military help to ward them off. This was granted. By 26 October, Maharaja Hari Singh of Kashmir had acceded to join India.

'I have been called a Kashmiri in the sense that ten generations ago my people came down from Kashmir to India. That is not the bond I have in mind when I think of Kashmir, but other bonds that have tied us much closer,' Jawaharlal said in a speech to Parliament in August 1952.

He could see that India needed to think ahead towards her future. So, he set up bodies that could come up with Five-Year Plans, especially for agriculture, power, industry and social services. Between 1951 to 1955, India produced 20 per cent more food grains. He built a large dam at Bhakra Nangal in Punjab, and another at Hirakud in Orissa, the longest in the world in 1956. The wisdom of these dams has since been disputed.

It was clear to Jawaharlal that India's problems would grow unless its villagers had happier lives. On Gandhi Jayanti, 1952, he launched fifty-five projects that were to cover 25,000 villages and over 1,60,00,000 people. Roads were to be built. Schools and hospitals were to be set up. Public health was to be improved. Waste land was reclaimed. Those landlords who had acres of land were made to share some of it by law, so that more people had land.

As he saw these programmes grow to cover a fifth of India or over a lakh of villages by 1955, the Prime Minister said, 'All over India, there are now centres of human activity that are like lamps spreading their light more and more in the surrounding darkness. This light must grow and grow until it covers the land.'

When Jawaharlal looked beyond India, into Asia, he saw people just like his own, some still ruled by foreign powers. He saw India as a link between the East and the West. Two years after 1947, Burma (now Myanmar), the Philippines, and Ceylon (Sri Lanka) were also independent.

Soon, the Dutch set Indonesia free. A war was raging in Vietnam. Chinese forces had moved into Tibet in 1950. Nine years later, the Tibetan leader, the Dalai Lama, sought refuge in India.

At a March 1947 conference in Delhi, Jawaharlal had said:

> *Strong winds are blowing all over Asia. Let us not be afraid of them, but rather welcome them, for only with their help can we build the new Asia of our dreams. Let us have faith in these great new forces and the dream which is taking shape. Let us, above all, have faith in the human spirit which Asia has symbolized for these long ages past.*

In October 1949, Nehru visited the United States of America. He enjoyed the hospitality of the Illinois farmers as much as he did his chats with New York cabdrivers. He was startled to watch little boys delivering newspapers every morning to earn some pocket money. Perhaps the high point of his trip was his meeting with Nobel prize-winning physicist Dr Albert Einstein at Princeton University.

In the 1950s, there was little political peace in Nepal. In 1954, Burma, Ceylon, Pakistan and Indonesia met at Colombo to discuss Asia and the world. The United Nations was then refusing to recognize communist China. This upset the twenty-four Afro-Asian nations that met at Bandung in Indonesia in April 1955.

That July, Jawaharlal visited Russia, then part of the Soviet Union. That country was already deep in a war of words and ideas with the US, also known as the Cold War. He liked the Russian five-year plans. He admired how they had improved their education system, provided health care for more people and sped up their economy. He realized then that though he appreciated what Marxism had done in the Soviet Union, democracy was right for India.

In 1962, Chinese troops invaded India and captured some land in what is now Arunachal Pradesh and in Ladakh. The war's first major skirmish was when China attacked Indian troops north of the McMahon Line, which marks the Sino–Indian boundary according to a pact between Britain and Tibet signed in Simla in 1914. The conflict spilled over to Aksai Chin, which connects Tibet and Xingiang, close to Ladakh.

Much of the fighting took place in harsh conditions, at altitudes of over 4,250 metres! The icy weather and uneven terrain made it tough for soldiers to battle face to face. Over 3,000 Indian troops lost their lives, while the Chinese lost over 700 men. On 20 November 1962, China declared a ceasefire.

The Prime Minister saw this war as a major blow to his foreign policy, especially since he had visited China in 1954, before the Bandung conference. Yet, Jawaharlal found much to admire in China, such as the way women were studying further and working more, or the care that children and young people were given.

As Jawaharlal travelled widely, he met some of those who were to make history, as he did. They included Chairman Mao Zedong of China, Pope Pius XII at the Vatican, Prime Minister Fidel Castro of Cuba, American President John F. Kennedy, British Prime Minister Winston Churchill and American civil rights leader Martin Luther King.

At the UN General Assembly in Paris in November 1948, Jawaharlal had said, 'May I say, as a representative from Asia, that we honour Europe for its culture and for the great advance in human civilization which it represents? May I say that we are equally interested in the solution of European problems; but may I also say that the world is something bigger than Europe, and you will not solve your problems by thinking that the problems of the world are mainly European problems? There are vast tracts of the world which may not in the past, for a few generations, have taken much part in world affairs. But they are awake; their people are moving and they have no intention whatever of being ignored or being passed by. It is a simple fact that I think we have to remember, because unless you have the full picture of the world before you, you will not even understand the problem, and if you isolate any single problem in the world from the rest, you do not understand the problem. Today I do venture to submit that Asia counts in world affairs. Tomorrow it will count more than today.'

By the time Jawaharlal passed away on 27 May 1964, his words proved to be true.

One person, one vote
India first went to the polls as a democracy in 1952. When did other countries first have universal suffrage or the right to vote for all eligible adults, regardless of race, gender, beliefs or social status?

The earliest country to grant limited universal suffrage to all those over twenty-five was the Corsican Republic, which existed only from 1755 to 1769! Other similar experiments took place in the Paris commune in 1871, and New Zealand (though it was still a British colony) granted women voting rights in 1893. In 1906, Finland granted all eligible citizens the right to vote and to stand for election, the first European country to do so.

When the US constitution was written in 1790, only white male property owners had the right to vote (a mere 10 to 16 per cent of its population). By 1850, almost all adult white men could vote. Twenty years later, all males—even former slaves—had voting rights. But in 1890, several US states adopted a literacy test to keep African-Americans from voting! Other states allowed those whose grandfathers had voted before 1870 to continue to vote.

It was only in 1920 that American women gained the right to vote. It took four more years for Native Americans to be granted both citizenship and voting rights. The US Voting Rights Act of 1965 protected the rights of minority voters. In 1971, all citizens over eighteen were allowed to cast their votes.

In Britain, women over thirty were given franchise in 1918. This was partially because women workers had proved to be so efficient, contributing much to the British war efforts in World War I. By 1928, the country adopted universal suffrage.

16 ✒ The Child is the Man

This is the story of a child who once stole a pen from his father's desk.

This is about a boy who was schooled in England, yet became an Indian Prime Minister.

This is a history of a man whose birthday on 14 November is celebrated as Children's Day throughout India.

★ ★ ★

When Jawaharlal was a child, he dreamt of a world where India stood tall and proud on the world stage. He did not know then that he would shape an independent India, alongside the Mahatma.

During his years of studying at school and college in England, he learnt that it was fine for a people to be different. That Asia could be as strong as European powers. That India could find its own voice though it was ruled by the British.

One of his favourite poems was by the Nobel laureate Rabindranath Tagore, from his *Gitanjali* published in 1910. Its words spell out the poet's dream for India, shared by Jawaharlal:

Where the mind is without fear and the head is held high;
Where knowledge is free;
Where the world has not been broken up into fragments by narrow domestic walls;
Where words come out from the depth of truth;
Where tireless striving stretches its arms towards perfection:
Where the clear stream of reason has not lost its way into the dreary desert sand of dead habit;
Where the mind is led forward by thee into ever-widening thought and action—
Into that heaven of freedom, my Father, let my country awake.

Jawaharlal learnt to fight for the causes he believed in, to march with the Mahatma even when his father did not approve at first. He was bold and brave as he led an independent India into the world, looking out for the needs of the poorest of its poor.

But through it all, one aspect of his life remained constant—his love for children. When ten-year-old Indira was at Mussoorie in the Himalayas, he began to write her a series of letters from Allahabad in 1928. In *Letters from a Father to his Daughter*, he wrote of when there were no men or women on an earth that was too hot for human life, of the rocks and fossils that reveal these times. Before the written word, rocks and mountains, seas, stars, rivers and deserts were the book of nature.

In his words, 'If you see a little round shiny pebble, does it not tell you something? How did it get round and smooth and shiny, without any corners or rough edges?' Through the book of nature, he taught Indira of a school without walls, where people once wrote on the bark of the Bhojpatra tree! And more, much more, before handwriting and printing presses made it easy to record new facts, even to share these with others. He wrote of languages and trade, of kings and temples, of Egypt and China.

As an Indian Prime Minister herself, Indira Gandhi wrote of these letters, 'They taught one to treat nature as a book. I spent absorbing hours studying stones and plants, the lives of insects and at night, the stars.'

Indira passed on Jawaharlal's ways of seeing to her granddaughter, Priyanka Gandhi Vadra. The latter wrote of her grandmother, 'Even a little walk in the garden with her was an adventure and an exploration, as she taught us to observe the swirls and textures in a little pebble and the myriad colours in a beetle's wing, and identify the stars in the sky.'

From adult to child, through the generations, Jawaharlal passed on his love for nature, the Indian people and a world at peace with itself. A caring person, his friends watched him help old women who were in trouble, without a second thought. Or he would secretly give money to those in distress. In the villages, he would remember to ask a peasant how his family was.

One day, the Prime Minister asked the peon in his office how much he earned each month. 'Rs 14 a month,' replied the peon. Horrified at this pittance, Jawaharlal ordered that peons' salaries should be hiked to Rs 30 monthly immediately, at least a rupee per day!

At home, Jawaharlal would often take his grandchildren—Rajiv and Sanjay Gandhi—for a piggyback ride. He loved to take them with him to visit his pets, the tiger cubs and panda bears from China, in the garden around Teen Murti Bhawan in Delhi, where he lived as the Prime Minister!

Every day, Jawaharlal would do some yoga before a breakfast of porridge. At the table, he was a good host. He enjoyed slicing fruit neatly and offering it to his guests. Before he went to his office, he would meet members of the public who had stories or complaints to share with him. Sometimes, when he had an official lunch at the Teen Murti garden, he could not resist showing his guests the pet pandas he so loved.

Whenever he needed a break, he would go away to the beautiful foothills of the Himalayas or the unspoilt woods far away from the city. He loved to be amidst birds, animals and plants.

Those who knew Jawaharlal saw how deeply he loved children. At public gatherings, he would throw his marigold garlands to them. He would sit cross-legged on the floor to listen to happenings at their school or tales their grandmothers had told them.

Jawaharlal often wore a red rose on his jacket. Some

people say he began to do so from the day that a child pinned one on him.

Over the years, he came to be known as Chacha Nehru, a favourite uncle to children across India. He thought of each bright young face as a light for the future of the country. He would meet thousands of children at rallies in Delhi on his birthday. He enjoyed their company as much as they did his. Children from Jaipur would send him handmade birthday cards in the 1960s. He would respond to each with a thank you note that he signed personally. Hundreds of Indian children in the 1950s and 1960s owned photographs of the Prime Minister handing over their prizes after a competition of drawing or writing.

Jawaharlal worked so hard that, by 1964, he was very tired. He flew to Dehradun for a holiday, then returned to Delhi cheerful and rested. But on the morning of 27 May, he felt too ill to get up. Doctors were summoned. Indira Gandhi rushed to his bedside. But he never woke up from that long day's sleep.

In his will, Jawaharlal wrote:

I am proud of that great inheritance that has been and is, ours, and am conscious that I too, like all of us, am a link in the unbroken chain that goes back to the dawn of history in the immemorial past of India. That chain I would not break, for I treasure it and seek inspiration from it. And as witness of this desire of my mind and as

my last homage to India's cultural inheritance, I am
making this request that a handful of my ashes be thrown
into the Ganga at Allahabad to be carried to the great
ocean that washes India's shores.

The major portion of my ashes should, however, be
disposed of otherwise. I want these to be carried high up
into the air in an aeroplane and scattered from that height
over the fields where the peasants of India toil, so that
they might mingle with the dust and soil of India . . .

At Shanti Vana, where he was cremated, thousands still pay their homage to the man who was Jawaharlal. At Teen Murti Bhawan, the constantly burning flame in his memory is called the Jawahar Jyoti.

From 1964 onwards, his birthday has been celebrated throughout India as Children's Day—a day to remember the first Prime Minister of India, who loved children as much as he loved his country.

How did Jawaharlal see himself? He once said, 'This was a man who, with all his mind and heart, loved India and the Indian people. And they in turn were indulgent to him and gave him their love abundantly and extravagantly . . .'

★ ★ ★

It was a long and winding road that took the child born at Anand Bhawan to his last steps as the Indian

Prime Minister at Teen Murti Bhawan. It was not an easy journey. He often had to remind himself of how much more he had to do with every breath he took.

By his bedside at Teen Murti, Jawaharlal had scribbled the lines of one of his favourite poems by the American poet Robert Frost. They read:

The woods are lovely, dark and deep,
But I have promises to keep,
And miles to go before I sleep,
And miles to go before I sleep . . .

TRIVIA
TREASURY

Turn the pages to discover
more fascinating facts and
tantalizing tidbits of history
about this legendary life
and his world.

WHAT HAPPENED AND WHEN

- **1889:** Adolf Hitler is born.
  - Japan enacts the Meiji Constitution, the country's fundamental law till 1947.
- **Early 1900s:** Marie Curie discovers Radioactivity.
  - Pablo Picasso creates Cubism.
- **1903:** Wright Brothers invent the airplane.
- **1905:** Albert Einstein advances his Theory of Relativity.
- **1907:** Australia and New Zealand gain independence from Britain.
- **1910:** Japan annexes Korea.
  - South Africa introduces apartheid.
- **1914:** Panama Canal opens.
  - World War I begins.
- **1917:** Bread riots in St. Petersberg turn into the Russian Bolshevik revolution against the Tsar Nicholas II of the Romanov dynasty. Lenin and Trotsky take over.
  - United States enters the war.
- **1918:** Armistice ends war. Germany agrees to it.
  - Influenza epidemic in the US kills over 20 million people.
- **1919:** Versailles peace conference.

- US President Woodrow Wilson outlines Fourteen Points for Peace.
- Germany signs peace treaty.
- **1920:** Woodrow Wilson awarded the Nobel Peace Prize.
- **1921:** Lenin introduces new economic policy in Russia.
- **1922:** New Communist constitution in Russia.
  - Soviet Union formed.
- **1923:** Kemal Ataturk beings to modernize Turkey.
- **1924:** Lenin dies.
- **1929:** The Great Depression begins.
- **1925:** Mussolini comes to power in Italy.
- **1926:** Three million British workers go on general strike.
- **1928:** Stalin proposes the Soviet Union's first five-year plan.
  - Russian peasants forced to give up land and work on collectives.
- **1930:** The Soviet Union becomes a totalitarian state.
- **1933:** Hitler becomes the Chancellor of Germany.
- **1934:** Mao Zedong leads the Long March in China.
- **1936:** Spanish Civil War begins, led by Francisco Franco.
- **1936–38:** Great Purge in the Soviet Union. Peasants, civilians and army people spied on by the police. Over 6,00,000 estimated deaths.
- **1937:** Japan invades China.
- **1938:** German Kristallnacht or Night of the Broken Glass in November. The persecution of German Jews begins.
  - Hitler takes over Austria.

- **1939:** World War II begins. Germany invades Poland. Nazis annexe Czechoslovakia.
- **1941:** Japan bombs Pearl Harbor, destroying nineteen ships, killing 2,400 people. The US enters the war.
- **1942:** The Axis Powers start to lose ground.
  - Gen. Dwight Eisenhower takes command of the US forces.
  - The Battle of Stalingrad begins.
- **1943:** Stalingrad surrenders.
  - D–Day: the Allied forces land on Normandy Beach in June.
  - Germany launches a counterattack at the Battle of Bulge.
- **1945:** US President F.D. Roosevelt, British Prime Minister Winston Churchill and Soviet Prime Minister Josef Stalin meet at Yalta in February.
  - First atomic bomb tested in Alamogordo, New Mexico.
  - Atomic bomb dropped on Hiroshima, 6 August.
  - Soviet Union declares war on Japan.
  - Atomic bomb dropped on Nagasaki, 9 August.
  - Emperor Hirohito forces the Japanese forces to surrender.
  - World War II ends.
  - President Roosevelt dies.
- **1946:** The 'Cold War' between the Soviet states and the Western powers begins. Churchill speaks of the 'iron curtain' between them on a visit to the US.

- **1948:** Palestine Liberation Organization formed.
  - Afrikaaner National Party wins a majority in South Africa's 'whites only' Parliament.
- **1949:** NATO (North Atlantic Treaty Organisation) comes into existence.
  - People's Republic of China founded.
- **1950:** North Korea invades South Korea.
- **1952:** US occupation of Japan ends.
- **1953:** Stalin dies.
- **1954:** Geneva Conference reaches accord on ending the war in French Indochina and Vietnam.
- **1955:** The Soviet Union and its allies sign a security agreement, the Warsaw Pact, in May. Under it, the forces of Poland, East Germany, Czechoslovakia, Hungary, Romania, Bulgaria and Albania agree to put their armed forces under a single command.
- **1957:** The Soviets launch Sputnik-1 into space.
- **1961:** A wall dividing east Berlin from the west, the Berlin Wall, comes up on 13 August.
  - John F. Kennedy becomes the US President.
- **1963:** First nuclear test ban treaty between the US, the UK and the Soviet Union signed in August.
  - President Kennedy assassinated in November.
- **1964:** Leonid Brezhnev assumes power in the Soviet Union.
  - US President Lyndon B. Johnson commits large numbers of American troops to the Vietnam war.
  - Nelson Mandela is sentenced to a life term in prison in South Africa.

TIME MARCHES ON IN INDIA

- **1905:** Earthquake near Kangra kills 20,000.
  - Partition of Bengal by Lord Curzon, the Viceroy. Reunification in 1911.
- **1906:** British India adopts Indian Standard Time.
  - Mahatma Gandhi coins the term satyagraha in South Africa.
  - All India Muslim League formed.
  - R.K. Narayan, novelist, born.
- **1911:** Henry Piquet flew a Humber biplane from Allahabad to Naini junction, carrying mail. It was the first flight in India.

  11 December: King George V and his wife Queen Mary have a formal coronation in Delhi as the Emperor of India and his Empress Consort.

  12 December: The capital of India is shifted from Calcutta to New Delhi.

  27 December: *Jana Gana Mana,* India's future national anthem, is sung for the first time at the Indian National Congress session at Calcutta.
- **1920:** Mohammedan Anglo-Oriental College in Aligarh, founded by Sir Syed Ahmed Khan in 1875, becomes Aligarh Muslim University.
- **1921:** Viswabharati University, set up by Rabindranath Tagore at Santiniketan, inaugurated.
  - Filmmaker Satyajit Ray born in Calcutta.

- **1924:** In Calcutta, Gopinath Saha is arrested for shooting a man he mistook for the city's Police Commissioner, Charles Augustus Tegart.
  - Netaji Subhas Chandra arrested and jailed for two and a half years.
- **3 February 1925:** India's first electric train travels from Victoria Terminus in central Bombay to Kurla.
  26 December: Communist Party of India founded at Kanpur.
- **15 July 1926:** BEST (Bombay Electric Supply and Transport) buses first run on Bombay roads.
- **1928:** Board of Control for Cricket in India formed.
- **1929:** Bombay Flying Club founded by J.R.D. Tata.
- **16 May 1932:** Hindu-Muslim riots in Bombay. Thousands dead and injured.
  20 September: Gandhi begins hunger strike in Poona prison.
  8 October: Indian Air Force established.
  15 October: J.R.D. Tata flies from Karachi to Bombay via Ahmedabad, landing on a grass strip at Juhu, the first Indian civil aviation flight.
- **7 April 1934:** Gandhi suspends civil disobedience campaign.
  - Earthquake in India and Nepal, measuring 8.4 on the Richter scale, kills over 10,000.
  - G. Edward Lewis discovers 'man-like ape' fossils in northern India. They are named *Ramapithecus* and *Sugrivapithecus*, after Rama and Sugriva.
  - The Reserve Bank of India Act passed.

- **3 May 1939:** Netaji Subhas Chandra Bose forms All India Forward Bloc.
- **7 August 1941:** Rabindranath Tagore dies at Jorasanko mansion, north of Calcutta, where he was born.
- **16 October 1942:** Hurricane and floods in Bombay. Over 40,000 dead.
  - Indira Priyadarshini Nehru marries Feroze Gandhi.
- **30 December 1943:** Netaji sets up a pro-Japanese Indian government at Port Blair in the Andamans.
- **1945:** Netaji allegedly dies in a plane crash in Taiwan
  20 August: Rajiv Gandhi born in Bombay.
  29 November: Bajaj Auto is registered.
- **19 August 1946:** Communal violence in Calcutta. Over 3,000 dead.
  4 September: Muslim–Hindu riots in Bombay.
  14 December: Sanjay Gandhi born in Bombay.
  - British Cabinet Mission to India.
  - Tata Airlines renamed Air India.
- **14 August 1947:** Pakistan is created.
  15 August: India gains independence from the British.
  - Rajendra Prasad becomes the first President, Jawaharlal Nehru the first Prime Minister.
  - Air India goes international.
  - Indo–Pakistani clashes in Kashmir.
- **30 January 1948:** Mahatma Gandhi assassinated by Nathuram Godse.
  12 September: Indian army enters Hyderabad in Operation Polo.
- **1949:** United Nations Security Council asks for ceasefire in Kashmir.

1 April: Reserve Bank of India established.

28 April: India issues London Declaration, which makes it possible for independent republics to remain in the Commonwealth.

15 November: Nathuram Godse and Narayan Apte executed for the Gandhi assassination.

- **25 January 1950:** Election Commission established.

26 January: Indian constitution comes into force. India becomes a republic.

15 August: Earthquake and floods in Assam: 574 deaths, over five million rendered homeless.

- **1951:** Central Railways comes into being, merging other government-owned railways.

16 December: Salar Jung Museum in Hyderabad opens to the public, displaying the fabulous collection of the Nizam.

- **13 May 1952:** Jawaharlal Nehru forms his first government.

15 May: G.V. Mavlankar takes charge as Lok Sabha's first speaker, with M. Ananthasayanam Ayyangar as his deputy.
  - India's first general election. Congress sweeps to power.
  - India's first Five-Year Plan tabled in the Lok Sabha.
- **1953:** Indian Airlines created.
  - Air India nationalized.
- **1954:** Bombay Electricity Board formed.
- **1955:** Imperial Bank of India, established in 1921, the subcontinent's largest commercial bank, transformed into the State Bank of India.

- **1956:** States Reorganisation Act passed, to redefine Indian states along linguistic lines.
- **17 March 1959:** Tenzin Gyatso, the 14th Dalai Lama, flees Tibet. He travels to India.
  - Doordarshan, India's first state broadcasting system, established.
  - Bajaj Auto given a licence to manufacture two and three-wheelers in India.
- **1960:** First Air India flight to the US touches down at New York.
- **17 December 1961:** India troops occupy Portuguese colonies of Goa, Daman and Diu.
  19 December: Goa officially cedes to India after 400 years of Portuguese rule.
- **10 October 1962:** Sino-India war begins.
  21 November: China withdraws troops, orders a ceasefire.
  19 December: Daman and Diu integrated into India Locust swarm threatens New Delhi.
- **27 May 1964 :** Jawaharlal Nehru dies. Lal Bahadur Shastri succeeds him as Prime Minister.
  - Viswa Hindu Parishad formed.

A SONG ABOUT CHACHA NEHRU

Though Jawaharlal Nehru passed away in 1964, his memory is kept alive in the minds of Indian children through songs like this one, which is still taught in schools across the Hindi-speaking belt:

Desh dulare jag ke pyare
Chacha Nehru bade saral the
Sevak jyada neta cum the
Bapu ke voh shishya parm the
Jinko paakar khush thi dharti
Duniya jinka aadar karti
Jeevan main jo kabhi na hare
Such dukh sab sehte, nishchal se
Pakshpat voh kabhi na karte
Shanti bhavna sabme bharte
Desh dulare . . .
Jinki sundar baatein sunkar
Nirbal bhi paa jaate bal the
Jahan jahan jaate chaa jaate
Bachchon main bhi ghul mil jaate
Tum bhi pran kar lo he mitron
Chacha se tum ban jaaoge
Desh dulare . . .

WHAT IS CIVILIZATION?

When Indira was just ten, she spent a summer vacation in Mussoorie. Her father, Jawaharlal, was busy in Allahabad and could not join her. Over those months, he wrote her a series of letters about the story of the earth, about evolution, civilization and society. His love for people, and for nature, comes through in these words. His words, written in 1928, ring true today:

I am going to tell you something about the early civilizations. But before I do so, we must try to form some idea of what civilization means. The dictionary will tell you that to civilize means to better, to refine, to replace savage habits by good ones. The savage condition of people when men were little better than beasts is called barbarism. Civilization is the reverse of that. The further away we get from barbarism, the more civilized we are.

But how can we find out if a person or a society is barbarous or civilized? Many people in Europe think that they are civilized and the people of Asia are quite barbarous. Is this because the people of Europe put on more clothes than the peoples of Asia and Africa? But clothes depend on the climate. In a cold climate men put on more clothes than in a hot climate. Or is it because a man with a gun is stronger than the man without a weapon and is therefore more civilized than him?

Whether he is more civilized or not, the man who is weak dare not tell him that he is not or else he might get shot!

You know that only a few years ago, there was a great war. Most of the countries of the world were in it, and every one of them was trying to kill as many people on the other side as possible . . .

. . . Do you think it was a very civilized or sensible thing for people to kill each other like this? . . .

So if you look at this question in this way you will say that the countries that fought and killed in the Great War—England, Germany, France, Italy and many others—are not at all civilized. And yet you know that there are many fine things and many fine people in these countries.

You will say that it is not easy to understand what civilization means, and you will be right. It is a very difficult question. Fine buildings, fine pictures and books and everything that is beautiful are certainly signs of civilization. But an even better sign is a fine man who is unselfish and works with others for the good of all. To work together is better than to work singly, and to work together for the common good is the best of all.

(From *Letters from a Father to his Daughter*, Puffin India, 2004)

BOOKS TO READ

Here are some books you can read if you wish to find out more about Jawaharlal Nehru and the independence movement:

1. *Letters from a Father to his Daughter* by Jawaharlal Nehru (Puffin India, 2004)
2. *The Discovery of India* by Jawaharlal Nehru (Oxford University Press, 2002)
3. *Glimpses of World History* by Jawaharlal Nehru (Jawaharlal Nehru Memorial Fund, 1982)
4. *Jawaharlal Nehru* by Frank Moraes (Macmillan, 1956)
5. *Jawaharlal Nehru: His Life and Times* (Exhibition brochure, Government of India, undated)
6. *Nehru for Children* by M. Chalapathi Rau (Children's Book Trust, 1967)
7. *Jawaharlal Nehru: An Autobiography* (Jawaharlal Nehru Memorial Fund, 1962)
8. *Thoughts* by Jawaharlal Nehru (Jawaharlal Nehru Memorial Fund, 1985)
9. *An Autobiography* by Jawaharlal Nehru (Jawaharlal Nehru Memorial Fund, 1980)
10. *Madame Ambassador: The Life of Vijayalakshmi Pandit* by Anne Guthrie (Harcourt Brace, 1962)
11. *The Scope of Happiness: A Personal Memoir* by Vijayalakshmi Pandit (Orient Paperbacks, 1981)

Other Books in the Series

Ashoka: The Great and Compassionate King
By Subhadra Sen Gupta

After the fierce battle of Kalinga, the victorious king stood in the middle of the terrible carnage he had wrought, in a battlefield filled with the dead and dying, and took a close look at what he had achieved . . .

The transformation that came over this king after one of his most significant victories at war made him into a legend forever. Ashoka the Great, the ruler of ancient India's largest kingdom, took the path of peace, tolerance, non-violence and compassion. He now addressed his subjects as a father would his children, and erected pillars that spread his thoughts throughout the land in the people's own language. He put their welfare above all else and worked towards that for the rest of his life. One of the most well-known symbols from India's history, the Ashoka chakra, now adorns India's national flag, and the lion capital from his pillars is our national emblem.

In this lively, engrossing account of Ashoka's life and the times, Subhadra Sen Gupta deftly brings him alive again from behind the swirling mists of time. It is a story about war, devotion and a king's love for his people, embellished with many details about Mauryan society, battle codes and even freaky food facts! Plunge into some of the most dramatic episodes of India's history with the *Puffin Lives* series and let the past speak to you like never before.

Other Books in the Series

Rani Lakshmibai: The Valiant Queen of Jhansi
By Deepa Agarwal

The elephant obediently sank on its knees, responding to its mahout's commands. Three men mounted it. A little girl came running up. 'Wait, I want to ride it too! I want to ride it too!' she clamoured. The men ignored her pointedly. Her father Moropant pulled her away. 'It's not in your destiny to ride elephants,' he said.

The girl's large eyes flashed. 'It's my destiny to ride ten. Wait and see, Baba!'

A little girl Manikarnika, with an uncanny sense of her own destiny, grew up to be none other than the brave queen of Jhansi, Rani Lakshmibai. Trained in horse riding and the martial arts from an early age, Manu was married to Gangadhar Rao, the Maharaja of Jhansi, when she was thirteen. Soon after her husband's death, the reins of the kingdom passed on to her, and she took up this responsibility undeterred and fearless. When Jhansi faced the danger of annexation, she fought against the British with unflinching courage, losing her life in the course of the battle. She has since become one of the most inspiring heroes of the freedom struggle and a much-admired role model.

Deepa Agarwal chronicles the life and times of this legendary character in a gripping narrative, drawing a colourful portrait of bravery. This riveting account also includes nuggets of information about the eventful year 1857, making for a fascinating read.